The Complete Guide to Airedale Terriers

Andrea Brown Berman

LP Media Inc. Publishing

Text copyright © 2019 by LP Media Inc.

All rights reserved.

No part of this book may be reproduced or transmitted in any form or by any means, electronic or mechanical, including photocopying, recording, or by an information storage and retrieval system - except by a reviewer who may quote brief passages in a review to be printed in a magazine or newspaper - without permission in writing from the publisher. For information address LP Media Inc. Publishing, 3178 253rd Ave. NW, Isanti, MN 55040

www.lpmedia.org

Publication Data

Airedale Terriers

The Complete Guide to Airedale Terriers ---- First edition.

Summary: "Successfully raising an Airedale Terrier dog from puppy to old age" --- Provided by publisher.

ISBN: 978-1-09669-533-2

[1. Airedale Terriers --- Non-Fiction] I. Title.

This book has been written with the published intent to provide accurate and authoritative information in regard to the subject matter included. While every reasonable precaution has been taken in preparation of this book the author and publisher expressly disclaim responsibility for any errors, omissions, or adverse effects arising from the use or application of the information contained inside. The techniques and suggestions are to be used at the reader's discretion and are not to be considered a substitute for professional veterinary care. If you suspect a medical problem with your dog, consult your veterinarian.

Design by Sorin Rădulescu

First paperback edition, 2019

TABLE OF CONTENTS

INTRODUCTION
The Airedale Terrier from A to Z 7

CHAPTER 1
Get Acquainted with the Airedale Terrier 10
Personality and Common Characteristics 11
Physical Characteristics 12
A Brief Airedale Terrier History Lesson 14

CHAPTER 2
Before You Buy an Airedale 16
What's All This Going to Cost? 19

CHAPTER 3
Buying vs. Adopting 20
Younger or Older? 20
Breeder, Rescue, or Shelter? 22
Rescue Organizations 23
Finding a Reputable Breeder 24
Choosing the Perfect Pup 27
Male or Female? 28

CHAPTER 4
Preparing for Your New Arrival 30
Choosing a Veterinarian 31
Who's in Charge Here, Anyway? 33
Introducing Your New Pet to Other Pets in the Home 34

CHAPTER 5
Hidden Household Dangers 36
Crates 37
Plants 37
Toys 38
Household chemicals 38
Foods 39

CHAPTER 6

Supplies for Your Dog ... 40
Crate ... 40
Food ... 41
Food and water bowls ... 42
Leashes and harnesses ... 42
Identification tags ... 43
Dog bed ... 43
Coat/Paw Protection ... 44
Toys ... 45
Poop bags/bag holders ... 46
Treats ... 47
Odor Neutralizer ... 47
Grannick's Bitter Apple Spray ... 47
Grooming Supplies ... 48
Dog car seats, harnesses, tethers, restraints ... 49
Fencing, dog gates ... 49
Emergency kit ... 50
Location, Location, Location ... 50
What's in a Name? ... 51

CHAPTER 7

Welcoming Your Airedale to His New Home ... 54
The Ride Home ... 54
First Night in His New Home ... 56
Congratulations! You're a Dog Parent! ... 61

CHAPTER 8

Where Are Your Manners? ... 62
Training Your Airedale Terrier ... 63
Welcome to Basic Training—Class Is Now in Session ... 64

CHAPTER 9

The Commands ... 68
The Sit Command ... 68
"OK" a.k.a. "Release" ... 69
The Down Command ... 70
The Stay Command ... 70
The Recall ... 72
The Heel Command ... 74

The Drop It Command 75
Physical and Mental Exercise 76

CHAPTER 10
The Importance of Socializing 78
Introducing Your Airedale to People, Places, and Things That Go
Bump in the Night 79
Puppy Socialization Classes 81
Socializing Your Older Airedale Terrier with Other Dogs . . . 81
Socializing Your Dog with People 84
Benefits of Doggy Day Care to Socialize Your Dog 86
How to Choose a Doggy Day Care Facility 88

CHAPTER 11
Surviving the Teen Years 90

CHAPTER 12
Do You Need a Professional Dog Trainer? 94
Finding the Right Professional Dog Trainer 96
Types of Dog Training 97
    Puppy Training Classes 97
Beyond Puppy Training Class 99

CHAPTER 13
Dealing with Unwanted Behavior - Your Dog's Bad Habits . 100
Chewing 101
Separation Anxiety 102
Digging 105
Barking at the Door 106
Jumping 108
Aggression 109

CHAPTER 14
Your Airedale Terrier's Health and Nutrition 110
Health Disorders 110
The Importance of Regular Veterinary Visits 111
Pet Insurance 112
Grooming Requirements 113
Your Airedale Terrier's Nutrition 115
Probiotics for Dogs 116
Airedale Terriers as Therapy Dogs 117

CHAPTER 15

Your Aging Airedale **120**
The Older Airedale's Health **121**
Simple Adjustments **123**
When It's Time to Say Good-bye **125**
The Beginning **127**

INTRODUCTION

Behold the Airedale Terrier: smart and sassy, cute and classy, bold and brassy...

Whether you've already set your sights on adding a member of this breed to your household, or you're just beginning to consider an Airedale, this book will offer the guidance you'll need to ensure that the dog you choose will meet everyone's expectations.

Within any breed, there are certain standards which are typical: appearance, temperament, general health and behavioral characteristics. BUT... that's where it all ends, because for the most part, the unknown factor in this equation is the owner.

A breeder can offer an overview of their dogs based on their own expertise and experience. That's understood. What they can't anticipate is YOU, because YOU are the one who will ultimately be responsible for guiding this dog toward becoming a well-mannered, respectful, long-time friend and loving companion. If you're ready and willing to do your homework, make a commitment that will last for the life of your dog, and combine love, sweat, and tears with all the joys that an Airedale Terrier can bring, then let's get started on your Airedale Adventure. It's like no other, but then again, neither are the rewards!

The Airedale Terrier from A to Z

The Airedale Terrier is at the top of the alphabetical list of dog breeds, but is it the top choice for you? Here are some A to Z considerations if you think an Airedale might be on your A-list:

Alpha Dog
That's you. Are you ready to assume the position of "benevolent dictator"? With positive reinforcement, the Airedale member of your household will flourish.

Breeder
Before buying, check the breeder's reputation, their dogs' lineage, possible medical/behavioral issues, and get references. Responsible

breeders want to know if you are the right person for their dog. Don't take it personally.

Confident
Airedales rarely take a submissive stance. They're not typically aggressive, but they won't be the first to back down.

Devoted
Their loyalty is legendary. Their well-developed instincts will alert you to trouble. If your Airedale doesn't like someone, you probably shouldn't either.

Energy
Airedales need lots of playtime, brisk walks, and mental stimulation. If they get bored, your furniture may suffer.

Funny
Airedales are the original "party animal." Their sense of humor is legendary.

Grooming
They're NOT hypoallergenic, and DO shed, but minimally. They will need to be brushed frequently, so plan to schedule grooming appointments.

Healthy
Typical life expectancy for an Airedale Terrier is 10 to 13 years.

Intelligent
They learn very easily.

Joy
If an Airedale Terrier is the right dog for you, expect abundant happiness in your home.

Kids
Airedales and kids are a match made in Heaven. This breed can be rambunctious, so be sure your child is tolerant.

Leader of the pack
At least they will try to convince you of that.

Manners
Early socialization with people and dogs will be a necessity for your Airedale. A little doggy etiquette goes a long way.

Nimble: Their agility can get them into trouble. They can open a banana, eat the inside, and leave the peel. (Personal experience here!)

Obedience training!!!
'Nuf said...

Prey
Airedales were bred to be rodent hunters in Merry Olde England, where they originated. Squirrels, mice, beware!

Quick
You'll need to stay one step ahead of them. They are ingenious at figuring things out.

Rescues
If an Airedale puppy seems too much of a challenge for you, consider adopting from an Airedale rescue organization. Many older Airedales need fur-ever homes. Their lower energy level and maturity may be better suited to some owners.

Size
Typically, 40 to 70 pounds.

Temperament
Loving, friendly, outgoing, energetic, stubborn, smart, protective, curious.

Unique
Every Airedale is unique. Use these guidelines accordingly.

Vibes
Airedales are sensitive creatures. If you're sad, they'll cuddle. If you're upset, they'll comfort. They are aces at reading you.

Work
Give them a job. They need to be busy.

EXcavate
Airedale Terriers enjoy digging, usually when bored. Protect your garden!

Yelling
You will gain nothing but a sore throat. A calm, firm voice is more effective.

Zest
The phrase "a zest for life" describes the Airedale's personality perfectly. If you're willing to put some effort into the proper training of this wonderful breed, you will be rewarded with a loving companion, miles of smiles, and happy memories that will last a lifetime.

CHAPTER 1
Get Acquainted with the Airedale Terrier

Think back to how you first became aware of the Airedale breed. Perhaps you just happened to be out for a walk, and noticed a very regal, confident-looking, high-spirited dog on the end of a leash, looking for all the world like it knew the answer to "What is the meaning of life?" Spunky, inquisitive, with an obvious twinkle in its eyes, this dog seemed to have a real presence. Or, as your grandma may have called it, chutzpah. The dog for you? Perhaps.

You may have first noticed the Airedale as a participant on a televised dog show competition. Yup, that big Terrier who seemed to thrill to the applause and the attention of the audience. Win or lose, for just those few moments in the ring, he totally knew that it was all about him. The dog for you? Possibly.

Could it be that your old Aunt Sally had an Airedale who, over the years, had become a family favorite? (During the late 1940s and early '50s, this breed saw a big surge in popularity.) Have those black-and-white pictures in old photo albums inspired your Airedale envy? The dog for you? Could be.

Whatever the reason you're considering an Airedale, it must be said: Airedales are not for everyone. It's entirely up to you to do the research and make an informed decision. We're here to help.

CHAPTER 1   Get Acquainted with the Airedale Terrier

Personality and Common Characteristics

Hunting dogs like to hunt. Working dogs like to work. Airedales? Let us start by saying they're members of the Terrier family. In general, the Terrier is considered to have a little (and sometimes, a lot) more courage and confidence than many other dog breeds. They possess dynamic personalities, they're expressive, and they can be downright stubborn at times. If your idea of the perfect dog is a breed commonly known as the Couch Potato, this should serve as a heads-up.

A brief summary of the Terrier class, provided by that venerable authority on all things dog, the American Kennel Club, is as follows: "Feisty and energetic are two of the primary traits that come to mind for those who have experience with Terriers. In fact, many describe their distinct personalities as 'eager for a spirited argument'. Owners and breeders know that Terriers are not considered to be world-class bullies by any means. A Terrier may not be the first one to instigate a canine confrontation, but he's usually not the first one to back down either.

The largest member of the Terrier group, Airedales are often referred to as the "King of Terriers," both in size and personality. They can be full of themselves, and they will usually try to convince everyone that they are, indeed, "Big Dog." Airedales are wonderful with children, loyal and loving companions, and can be amazing watchdogs. Their dedication to their family is second to none. In the Airedale world, attitude is everything. But inside this stoic, charismatic, independent facade is a most intelligent, loyal, and loving dog. The Airedale has a finely tuned sense of humor, and will keep you constantly amused with his antics. His adorable, mischievous grin lets everyone know that he's a comic at heart, and always laughing. Sometimes WITH you, sometimes AT you.

> **FUN FACT**
>
> During WWI, Lieutenant Colonel Edwin Hautenville Richardson of Scotland was instrumental in introducing working dogs into the British military. Richardson and his wife Blanche eventually set up the British War Dogs training school in Shoeburyness, Essex. While Richardson trained a number of different breeds, he believed the Airedale was an ideal dog for military work. During the war, Airedales performed tasks such as transporting medical supplies for the Red Cross, carrying messages to soldiers on the front lines, and guard duties.

Photo Courtesy of Peter Hilton

Physical Characteristics

Within the Terrier group, there runs a gamut of size, appearance, and personalities. Airedales fall into the "medium" size category. Their weight is between 40 and 70 pounds, with males tipping the scale on the higher end. They are approximately 23 inches in height, give or take a few. They are not maintenance-free, but most owners find that a few thorough brushings a week and a visit to a professional groomer 3 or 4 times a year will suffice, at a minimum. Their coat is best described as wiry or coarse, although as a youngster, the Airedale's coat is somewhat soft and fluffy.

CHAPTER 1 Get Acquainted with the Airedale Terrier

Have you heard that the Airedale is a hypoallergenic dog and doesn't shed? Let us immediately put those rumors to rest. Shedding may not be a major concern for those who are not allergic to dogs; however, the Airedale does indeed shed—just not as badly as some other breeds. Sure, you won't be vacuuming up as much doggy fur as you would with a breed known to be a notorious shedder—a German Shepherd, for example. But count on your Airedale to most likely shed.

> **FUN FACT**
> **History Lesson**
>
> Airedales were originally bred by farmers to hunt game, both in and out of water. In order to preserve the hunting abilities in the breed, the Airedale Terrier Club of America (ATCA) formed the Hunting/Working Committee (HWC) in the mid-1980s. In 1986, the HWC held its first national Hunting Working Weekend in Ohio in order to test the Airedale's skills in three categories: hunting fur, water fowl, and upland birds.

If you are at all worried that your allergies may act up in the presence of an Airedale, please, please, please find out if this is the case well ahead of time. If you already have a breeder in mind, ask if you can schedule an appointment to hang out with their dogs for a little while. (No reputable breeder should refuse this request.) See if your eyes begin to water, or if you're showing any signs of even a small allergic reaction. It's not a good fit if every time your pup comes 'round for a snuggle, you sneeze in his face.

Photo Courtesy of Carly Kanipe

Photo Courtesy of Janis Bailey

It's quite clear that particular characteristics—both physical and behavioral—must certainly be considered when choosing any dog, but perhaps even more so when you KNOW what you can expect. There are exceptions to every rule, and not all dogs, even those from the same breeder, will exhibit the identical appearance and/or temperament as its littermates or even its close relatives. But with a little research, you'll have substantial information on which to base your decision. It's a decision which will likely affect your life, your pet's life, and the lives of everyone in your family for many years to come. Before you let your emotions take hold, as in, "OH! He's just precious! I WANT this dog!", be sure he's the RIGHT dog. And be sure you're the RIGHT dog parent.

General physical and behavioral characteristics aside, we are assuming that the Airedale Terrier which ultimately finds its way into your heart and home, no matter how gorgeous or handsome he or she is, will be destined for a lifetime of companionship rather than showmanship. If, however, you do plan on showing your dog professionally, we would highly recommend that before purchasing, you become familiar with standards, rules, regulations, and certifications which may be needed for your dog to participate and succeed in competitive events.

A Brief Airedale Terrier History Lesson

More than 50 of our most popular dog breeds today have their origins in Merry Olde England, including the Airedale Terrier. But unlike some of the oldest known breeds such as the Chinese Shar-Pei, the Basenji, and the Chow Chow, which date back to ancient times, the Airedale's history is much more recent. In the mid-1800s, hunters in the manufacturing town of River Aire Valley in Yorkshire, England,

Photo Courtesy of Carly Kanipe

CHAPTER 1 Get Acquainted with the Airedale Terrier

crossed the Black and Tan Terrier with the Otterhound. The combination of natural instincts from both these breeds—the ability of the Black and Tan to hunt rodents, and the extraordinary swimming and scenting skills of the Otterhound, produced the first incarnation of the Airedale Terrier. It is noted that additional breeds may have been added to the mix as well. These were thought to include Irish Terriers and Retrievers, to name but a few. The Airedale Terrier as we know it today soon landed on the shores of the USA. As early as 1888, the breed was officially recognized by the American Kennel Club. And the rest, as they say, is history. Over the years, the Airedale breed has gained worldwide respect, notability, and even celebrity status:

- Airedales were widely used in the military to carry messages to troops, especially during the First World War. Subsequently, they were also used as rescue dogs, as well as by law enforcement officials.
- In 1949, Airedales were listed in the "Top 20 Most Popular Dogs" by the American Kennel Club.
- The Airedale was the presidential pet of Theodore Roosevelt, Calvin Coolidge, and Warren G. Harding.

The Airedale Terrier, although not as popular as in years past, ranked a very respectable sixtieth out of 192 dog breeds registered by the American Kennel Club in 2018. They still have quite a large fan base, to which anyone who has ever owned one will attest.

Photo Courtesy of Joel Drolet

Photo Courtesy of Ruth Antoniuk

CHAPTER 2
Before You Buy an Airedale

"When looking for the right Airedale, consider your lifestyle, and routine. Do you have other dogs? Do you have a fenced yard? Do you have kids? How will you exercise your dog? Answering questions like this can give you a picture of what dog you need. Do you need a strong willed, energetic, alpha? Or do you need a more submissive, laid back personality? Or somewhere in between? Express these answers to the breeder, they know their dogs and puppies and have spent way more time with them, and their parents. Trust their input!"

Anne Ramseyer
Annes Airedales LLC

CHAPTER 2   Before You Buy an Airedale

If you've come to the conclusion that an Airedale Terrier is definitely the dog for you, your family, and your living situation, then what's the next step? Three words: research, research, research! OK, we lied. It's one word, but hopefully we've gotten our point across. It's incumbent upon you to choose the perfect dog, so here are a few points to ponder: Do you have children, a spouse, or a partner who would be able and willing to help out, or would you be the primary caregiver? Are you working outside the home, and if so, able to afford to pay someone to come in at regular intervals during the day to spend time with your dog and take him out? Is everyone agreeable to the idea of adding a pet to the household? If you are a renter, have you received permission from your landlord to have a pet? Is there a fenced-in area where your dog can safely be let out alone? Do you have other pets in the home who may not get along with another animal? What about noise? Would a barking dog be a disruption if you work at home or have neighbors close by?

FUN FACT
Adoption Statistics

According to the American Society for the Prevention of Cruelty to Animals (ASPCA) 3.2 million animals are adopted from shelters annually, half of which are dogs.

Can you afford to feed this new pet a quality diet? What about veterinary costs? Even with a healthy, older dog, there are booster shots, lab work, microchipping, flea and tick and heartworm medications, and costs associated with regularly scheduled check-ups to consider. Will you be spaying or neutering your dog?

Are you planning to take your dog to a doggy day care facility to socialize and get exercise? What about grooming expenses and the cost of an obedience trainer? And if your lifestyle includes travel, whether for business or pleasure, where will your canine companion stay when you are away and what will it cost? What about the equipment you'll need for your dog—a crate, dog gate, bedding, leashes, toys? Depending on your circumstances, there may be other expenses which can be costly, such as the installation of a fence.

Yes, there's a great deal to think about before you go ahead and bring that dog home, but one of the most important questions to ask yourself, in addition to all of the above, is...What about the time involved? For most of us, there are never enough hours in the day to take care of ourselves, our families, and our jobs. No matter how much you would love having a dog, could it possibly become a cause of unnecessary stress for you or

Photo Courtesy of Colleen Standley

CHAPTER 2   Before You Buy an Airedale

your household members? If you can honestly answer that you are all on board, and ready, willing, and able to take on the responsibility of pet ownership, no matter what the cost—physically, emotionally, and financially—then your next step is to find the perfect Airedale!

What's All This Going to Cost?

The rewards of dog ownership are limitless: the love, the companionship, the comfort of knowing that, no matter what, you've got a friend. All that is certainly priceless, but what's the care of a dog actually going to cost? Prices will vary depending upon location, needs, and options. You can buy the premium-priced brand of everything from a sheepskin-lined, monogrammed doggy bed, to the standard, polyester-filled, all-purpose variety. Your Airedale will most likely be just as happy with the no-frills version, but your standards might be a bit higher.

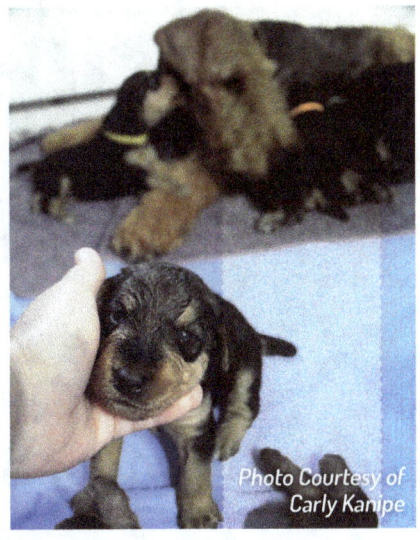
Photo Courtesy of Carly Kanipe

It's difficult to estimate how much money your dog will cost on an annual basis, but the first year of ownership will typically be more expensive than subsequent years. An expenditure of $1,500 to $2,000 would be considered average here in the Northeast, but may vary in other parts of the country. That, of course, does not include the price of the dog if you're purchasing from a breeder, where the cost could be $1,000 or more. The initial fee for dogs coming from a shelter or rescue organization will vary, depending upon the dog's age and other factors, but often the price can be $500, more or less.

Veterinary care, food, training, equipment, and day care/dog sitters will all add to the bottom line, and remember that there may be unforeseen and unexpected costs, which will increase your annual expense. If you're hesitant as to whether or not an Airedale Terrier may break your budget, do the numbers. Check with veterinary practices, day care facilities, and pet stores, and interview trainers to see whether a dog is a realistic financial investment for you.

CHAPTER 3
Buying vs. Adopting

Younger or Older?

Now that you've gotten over the "sticker shock" of dog ownership, it's time to consider the when, where, and how of acquiring the Airedale that best suits your lifestyle. Consider these questions: Are you up for the challenge of raising a very young, rambunctious pup who is clueless about housetraining, walking on a leash, good manners, and sociability? Are you physically able to care for an energetic dog who can go from 0 to 60 in the blink of an eye? Or would an older, more mature dog be a better fit for you and your family?

We have already mentioned that Airedales and kids are the proverbial "match made in Heaven," but would your children be timid around a frisky puppy with a penchant for nipping and play-biting? Kids and puppies are great company for each other, and they will surely tire each other out, but

CHAPTER 3   Buying vs. Adopting

we'd put our money on having the child's energy run out much sooner than that of a very active doggy youngster. Despite promises like, "Mom, I PROMISE to feed and walk him! Can we get a dog? Can we? PLEEEEASE??", if your child is like most, the responsibility angle gets old pretty quickly. Caring for a mature dog may be much more agreeable when a child has to balance baseball practice, homework, dance classes, and play dates. As a child parent and pet parent, it's up to you to decide whether an older or younger dog will be the best fit for your family.

> **FUN FACT**
> **To microchip or not to microchip?**
>
> According to the Humane Society of the United States, it's a good idea to both microchip your dog as well as make sure that your dog has an up-to-date tag on his or her collar. Microchips are simple to have implanted, but they can only be read by special scanners. Because most private citizens don't own microchip scanners, having tags on your dog's collar is a great way to make sure you are reunited with your dog quickly if it should become lost.

Is there anyone living in your home with a disability, and would it be putting them at risk for a puppy to be zipping around them at lightning speed? On the other hand, would a large dog be endangering a family member who may be in frail health? You may think that a new puppy could be that extra little spark that the older member of your household needs to keep them active and involved, but an older, more mature dog could offer the companionship and exercise they both need at this stage in their lives.

That's not to say that there isn't some middle ground here, so consider this compromise when deciding upon puppy versus older dog: What about the Airedale that may require a little additional effort on your part as well as his, but will reward you with many years of joy? He's not a young pup, he's not a wise old elder, but somewhere in between. He may have a few not-so-desirable habits, or through no fault of his own found himself in a bad living situation, but with a little loving care, could be just the ONE for you and your family. Death, divorce, jobs, and relocation happen, as we all too often find out. Someone else's cast-out canine could be your next best buddy, so there's one more option in your search for your dream dog.

Breeder, Rescue, or Shelter?

Photo Courtesy of Betsy Burroughs

Benefits and drawbacks abound here, and can vary exponentially. There are several choices, so let's start with the shelter. You'll find plenty of homeless waifs here, both mixed and pedigree, ranging in age from youngsters to gray-faced seniors. It's estimated that approximately 25% of dogs turned in to shelters are purebreds, so there's always a chance that you'll find an Airedale in a shelter. However, many purebred dogs who arrive in shelters will then go to an appropriate breed rescue.

You may never know the real circumstances of how a dog arrived at a shelter. Was it because an owner was unable—or unwilling—to care for him? Was it because of a death, a move, or a change in someone's household situation? There are as many reasons as there are dogs. Some owners of purebred dogs are unwilling to consult with the breeder from whom the dog was purchased, whether it's because they are embarrassed to admit that there may be a problem, or because they were unaware that this is an option. Perhaps the dog was a stray, found wandering the streets. Shelter workers and volunteers want to know that their dogs are being placed in the right home, and these kindhearted folks will do everything they can to ensure a perfect match.

If you do find a purebred Airedale in a shelter, you will most likely be asked to undergo a thorough background check. Don't be put off. It's in everyone's best interest, and whether you get your Airedale Terrier at a shelter, a rescue, or from a breeder, you will need to offer proof that you will be a responsible owner, capable of providing a safe, loving environment for that dog. You may be asked for income and residency verification, prior dog ownership experience, and how much time you can devote to being a dog parent. Do you own or rent your home? Will your landlord allow pets? If you own a home, you will need to present utility or tax bills in your name. If you have other pets, you might be asked to return to the shelter with them to make sure they will get along with the prospective newcomer.

A reputable shelter will also require you to have everyone in the household come in to meet the dog. Avoiding potential problems greatly reduces the chance that a dog will be returned. A good fit for the family is just as important as a good fit for the dog. Most shelter organizations will require you to have the shelter dog spayed or neutered by a certain age, or will spay and neuter before the dog goes to a new home.

Unfortunately, since most shelters are overcrowded it can sometimes be difficult to get a great deal of specific information on any one dog's personality traits. Volunteers at shelters may have some knowledge as to which dog needs a single-pet household, or which ones love kids and cats, or have some previous behavioral history, but even this can be vague, at best—attributable to so many homeless dogs, and so little time for shelter workers to devote to each and every one of them. It is indeed wonderful to find your dream dog at a shelter, but future pet parents must recognize and realize that shelter dogs may have some quirks at best, or just a sad story that accompanies what could be the most amazing dog you've ever known.

Rescue Organizations

Most dog pedigrees these days have breed rescues, which can, for a potential owner, be the right solution between shelter and breeder. Rescue workers and volunteers are likely to be very familiar with the breed. Whether the dogs which were turned in are housed in group kennels or, as is usually the case, foster homes, their caregivers know their personalities well, and can evaluate their physical and behavioral characteristics. Foster parents of canines waiting for adoption get to know their dogs, and are able to give wonderful insight as to what will ultimately lead to a successful adoption.

With both shelters and rescue organizations, you can expect a placement fee, but it may be less than acquiring a puppy from a breeder, depending upon the age, availability, and temperament of their dogs. There are quite stringent guidelines on dog placement, and these can fluctuate depending upon the organization. Submitting applications, providing references, scheduling home visits, spaying and neutering, vaccinations, and more will be dependent upon the rescue's criteria for adoption.

Rescue volunteers and foster families are located in many states, work diligently to have their dogs placed in the right home, and rely on donations and adoption fees to sustain their organizations. There are many great Airedale Terriers of every age waiting to find their forever homes, so if you haven't already thought about adopting, we encourage you to do a little investigative work and see if this option is right for you. Who knows? Your Airedale Terrier could be just a phone call or a keyboard stroke away!

Finding a Reputable Breeder

If you've made up your mind that a puppy is the best choice, where do you start? We will most emphatically offer this advice of where NOT to start: DO NOT start at the neighborhood pet store. Spending an hour or two in a small room playing with a dog may be a nice way to pass the time, and your salesperson will try to tell you all the reasons why you NEED this dog, and the fact that, "This week only, she's on sale, plus we'll include the price of her first vet visit, a beautiful red and white New England Patriots collar, and her first bag of dog food. Don't wait, because we have someone else who's interested in her!" If you think you're "rescuing" this dog from a glass-enclosed 3-foot-by-3-foot cage, and that you're doing a good thing, you're really only making room for another dog from another commercial, for-profit puppy factory. You will end up paying the price of the pet store's overhead, you don't know where the dog came from, are unfamiliar with its family history/lineage from a temperament standpoint, and all too often, there are unseen health issues. In the long run, a pet store puppy could cost you much more than getting a dog from a reputable breeder. 'Nuff said on that subject.

How do you find a reputable Airedale breeder? Start by checking with your local veterinary practice, but don't stop there. Talk to strangers (well, the ones walking Airedales anyway!). Ask for referrals. Ask questions. Is their dog healthy? What's the temperament? Do they know the breeder personally? Make phone calls and email inquiries, and don't commit to the first breeder you find. Chances are you might be put on a wait list, so pull up your big girl pants, be patient, and try to understand that you probably won't be taking home a dog in a matter of days, weeks, or even months. In the long run, it will all be worth it.

An excellent resource is the ATCA—Airedale Terrier Club of America. Find it online at airedale.org. With an extensive list of member/breeders, the ATCA offers a wealth of knowledge and listings of breeders by state. There are also many other internet sites which may be helpful including various Facebook pages pertaining to breeders and associations. Check local breeders' clubs. They can offer help with referrals.

A few tips when trying to discern which breeder is right for you: Visit the facility. Ask questions. Ask for references and verify that they are credible. Interact with the dogs on the premises. Check to see that the environment is clean. Ask to see the parents of your prospective dog. Request to see certifications, registrations, AKC pedigrees, and health reports. Inquire about any genetic issues. (This is extremely important!) Read contracts and war-

CHAPTER 3 Buying vs. Adopting

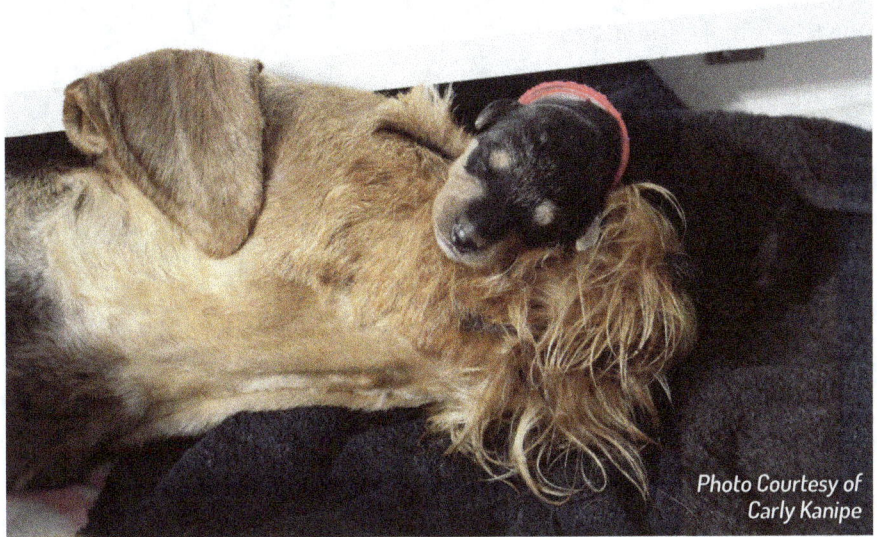

Photo Courtesy of Carly Kanipe

rantees before you sign, and become familiar with the obligations of both the buyer and the breeder. Be prepared for the breeder to interview you.

It should be noted that there are several categories of breeders: professional breeders, hobby breeders, and the "backyard breeders." Hobby breeders are conscientious, responsible breeders who, rather than producing large litters, are more interested in working to perpetuate a particular lineage. The quality of their dogs is as important to them as it is to a professional breeder, and they are ethical, knowledgeable, hardworking people, dedicated to their particular breed.

Stay away from the backyard breeder. They are often only a step up (and in some cases, a step or two down) from the pet stores and puppy mills. They are in the business for one thing, and one thing only—profit. You'll find them advertising throughout the internet, and while they may try to convince you that they always put the health and welfare of their dogs first, it's far from the truth. Don't be fooled by empty promises. A reputable breeder will want to be sure that their dogs will be placed in the perfect household. If it's a good match from everyone's point of view, you'll have taken the first steps on the path to finding the right dog for you and your family.

Personal note: Here's a story about a good friend of mine—a very gullible, foolish, and somewhat impulsive young lady...OK, I'm lying here. It was me. Many years ago, prior to becoming a professional dog trainer, I was walking along one of the many lovely beaches of Boston's North Shore, when I spotted the most magnificent dog running along the water's edge. He was huge, hairy, and handsome, and immediately came to greet me with wet kisses and a wagging tail. Dog lovers make friends easily, and this dog's owner and I began chatting. "He's a Bernese Mountain Dog. He loves everyone. Best dog I've ever had."

The owner, Frank, and I quickly became friends and realized that we lived nearby one another. Frank brought "Moose" around to visit often, and I soon decided that my next dog would be a Berner. Sadly, Frank passed away before I thought to ask about his breeder. But now I was a woman on a mission. I wanted—no, needed—a dog just like Moose.

Photo Courtesy of Sunny Vellios

This all took place before we had such impressive inventions as web sites, blogs, and Google, so other than email (think CompuServe; yes, this was the dark ages of the internet) I was pretty much on my own. After many hours of research, I managed to locate a breeder of Bernese Mountain Dogs who was in nearby Vermont, "only" a mere 3½ hour drive from my home. I chatted extensively with the breeder via telephone, as she informed me that she had 2 pups for sale, a male and a female, from her current litter. They were 12 weeks old and ready to go. The price was within my budget, and although I was willing to make the 3½ hour drive, she "coincidentally" was driving a little bit south to drop off one of the dogs to another buyer, and would I like to meet her and have first choice? Oh, and by the way, it would have to be a cash transaction.

It all sounded well and good to me, so we arranged to meet. The halfway point was the parking lot at Burger King in Brattleboro, Vermont. (Do we see any red flags here?) We rendezvoused at the appointed time, and a woman soon exited an SUV with 2 small dog crates, each containing the most adorable balls of black, brown, and white fluff I had ever seen. The female pup and I bonded immediately, so there was no doubt in my mind that I had found "MY" dog. The breeder said that since she was not sure which dog I would want, she would have to send me the AKC certificates and all

CHAPTER 3   Buying vs. Adopting

of the vet records as soon as she returned home, but assured me that her dogs were healthy and from an excellent lineage. Who was I to doubt her?

Fast forward to a few months in the future, and you can probably guess what happened. Despite calling many times, I received no response from the breeder, no certificates, nothing in writing. Nada, zippo, zilch. Moxie was, indeed, the beautiful, loving dog that I had wanted. What I hadn't wanted was the vet bills that ensued. Hip dysplasia, elbow dysplasia, food allergies, skin, eye, and ear issues. With a little luck, a lot of money, and often weekly trips to the vet, she managed to reach the age of 11, almost unheard of for a Berner. She was greatly loved and our years together were filled with some very happy memories, despite her sad health history and my empty wallet.

What did I learn from this experience? There are good breeders and then there are "backyard breeders"—the ones who are only interested in making a few bucks at the expense of a very naive dog lover. Caveat emptor. Let the buyer beware.

Choosing the Perfect Pup

An experienced, reputable breeder will have a thorough knowledge of their dogs, their dogs' history, and any potential health issues, and they will want to be sure that their dogs will be placed in the right home situation. A dog who must be returned for ANY reason is one dog too many. But a good, responsible breeder should be willing to try to alleviate any problems that may arise, answer questions, and, if need be, take a dog back. Certainly every situation is different, but it is the responsibility of the buyer to get everything in writing, ask questions, and be sure that you are agreeable to all terms of the contract before you sign. Whether or not you will be entitled to some, all, or none of your money will be up to the breeder and the individual situation. Every breeder and buyer hopes that this will never happen, but there can be unforeseen circumstances.

Breeders, for the most part, encourage their dogs' owners and prospective owners to stay in contact, and would much rather spend time answering questions, offering assistance, and making sure that their dogs are happy and healthy, than having to re-home one of their dogs. If there are concerns of any kind, from the most innocuous quirky behavior to a potentially problematic situation, contact your breeder. And if your pup is just the love of your life and is everything you'd hoped it would be, let the breeder know that, too. Kudos to all the great, caring breeders out there!

Male or Female?

Despite years of research, it appears that no one has yet to figure out if there is an advantage to owning one gender of dog over another. Really, it all boils down to personal preference, so we can't offer a definitive answer to this question. If, for example, you've always had female dogs, or feel that you can relate better to one gender more than another, then your decision will be easier. If you think male dogs are more your cuppa tea, you most likely have your own valid reason. So the advice here would be stick with that with which you're comfortable.

There are many stereotypical, age-old arguments for why you should or shouldn't get one gender of dog or the other, and you'll hear all sorts of differing opinions. I have owned dogs my entire adult life, both male and female, and although the females have outnumbered the males, I've loved them all the same. In most breeds, a male will usually be a bit larger than a female, and Airedales are no exception.

Temperament-wise, I have had a few female dogs who were more assertive than males. There are some behavioral issues that can be inherent in both genders. Females may be viewed as typically more gentle, but I can state here in no uncertain terms that it's not always the case. My first dog was a male Cocker Spaniel who, if you looked at him the wrong way, would submissively squat, pee on your shoe, and tremble in fear of some unknown demon about to emerge from under his doggy bed. My female Airedale, on the other hand, well, let's just say "quite outgoing" would be a fitting description for her personality.

Other than temperament, there are a few additional considerations. Males who are not neutered may have more of a tendency to roam. In some breeds, unneutered males may be considered to be more assertive. If you are not planning to spay a female dog, you must take into consideration whether or not you are prepared to deal with her going into heat. Many male dogs will urinate frequently to mark their territory when being walked or even in the home. But there is the occasional female who does this also. Six of one, half a dozen of the other. An experienced breeder who spends weeks and months with their dogs can advise you on their particular personality traits so listen to their guidance. Unless you've already decided on male vs. female, quiet and laidback vs. Ms. Happy-Go-Lucky-Party-Animal, then keep an open mind. Often, it's not you who will choose the dog, but the dog who will choose you!

CHAPTER 3 Buying vs. Adopting

Photo Courtesy of
Susannah Bell

Photo Courtesy of Angela Lockett

CHAPTER 4
Preparing for Your New Arrival

The original title of this chapter was "Preparing Your Home for Your New Arrival," but we thought long and hard and decided that it was not only the home that needed preparing. It also needed to include the PEOPLE (and other pets) in that home. Is everyone ready for this new adventure? Think about bringing a new baby home from the hospital. You've been preparing for 9 months, and that squirming, cuddly, precious baby will need a warm place to sleep, appropriate feeding supplies, clothing, a stack of diapers, cuddly toys, and all the accoutrements that go along with this little bundle of joy. And, of course, a family who is committed to welcoming, caring for, and loving the new addition.

Even with all the preliminary work done, no amount of preparation can foretell what's about to launch your household into the uncharted experience of adding another member to your previously safe and sane environment. Likewise, you can't just bring home a new dog and expect life to be all rainbows and unicorns from the get-go. Whether that new family member is a puppy, an older dog, or a gray-muzzled senior, some preplanning is necessary. Let the fun begin!

CHAPTER 4   Preparing for Your New Arrival

Choosing a Veterinarian

If you already have pets, and a veterinarian you'll be taking your new dog to, that's one item you can check off your "to-do" list. If you're in need of how to go about choosing a vet, we have some suggestions. Begin the process by asking all of your dog parent friends for referrals, and the reasons why they take their dogs to that particular veterinary practice. Listen to the answers and decide for yourself what your priorities are.

For instance, one neighbor may have chosen a certain vet because the practice has extended hours to include early morning, late night, or weekend appointments. If your work schedule is inflexible, take this into consideration. Some dog owners would rather use a small veterinary practice, where the same vet will usually be on duty and will become familiar with the dog. Other dog owners would prefer a larger practice, where, in case of emergency, there is a better chance of getting medical care immediately, whether or not that doctor is one who routinely sees the dog.

Location should also be an important consideration when choosing a vet, because: (a) emergencies happen and (b) frequent visits also happen. Cousin Charlotte may have been bringing Fluffy to Dr. Smith for years, but if Dr. Smith's office is an hour away from where you live, it may not be a good choice for you.

If you don't know anyone in your area who can give you some guidance as to which vet to see, many towns have Facebook or neighborhood-based web pages where you can ask for recommendations. I have used my community's page to find referrals for everything from plumbers to acupuncture, and have always been impressed with the number of helpful people who are willing to share their best endorsements. (Of course, do NOT give out any information to anyone you do not personally know. Just a word of internet caution, sprinkled with a bit of common sense.)

On the other hand, if someone tells you NOT to see a certain vet, ask why, and what the extenuating circumstance might have been. Could it have been a personal issue? Financial? Ethics? Personality? People hold grudges for reasons big and small,

Photo Courtesy of
Madeleine Horn
Bred by DogwoodDales of Sherman, Texas

Photo Courtesy of Linda Schrieks

so determine what's best for you and your dog.

Choose several potential veterinary practices, and make appointments to visit before your new dog comes into your home. First impressions are important. Is the practice clean and sanitary? Is their equipment up to date? What about the general atmosphere? Is the staff helpful and welcoming? Do they see many Airedale Terriers and are they familiar with possible health and genetic issues that may be inherent in the breed? If you're planning to adopt an older dog, is the practice specialized or equipped to deal with geriatric dogs? If you have specific concerns, such as organic nutrition and/or holistic treatment, are they knowledgeable? Ask for a schedule of when your dog should be seen for his first and subsequent visits, and an estimate of what the charges will be for regular visits, immunizations, lab work, and annual testing. If you're planning to subscribe to pet insurance, is the veterinary practice you select within the coverage network, and do you know what types of claims the insurance will cover?

A few more considerations when choosing a vet: Is the practice equipped to handle emergencies or will you be referred elsewhere? What type of payments are acceptable? (Some vets will not accept checks or certain credit cards.) In an emergency, will you have the necessary means to pay for your dog's treatment? Extensive treatment can run into thousands of dollars. What is the average wait time to schedule a routine appointment? Will it be same day, same week, or a month away?

There's a lot to consider when choosing a veterinary practice, but planning ahead can alleviate potential problems. Weigh the pros and cons. And listen to your intuition. Our gut instincts are seldom wrong!

CHAPTER 4   Preparing for Your New Arrival

Who's in Charge Here, Anyway?

Before your new Airedale arrives, determine who the primary caregiver in your home will be. If dog care is to be shared equally by adults only, decide who will be responsible for feeding, walking, purchasing supplies, vet visits, day care, and daily necessities. We're assuming (and hoping) that everyone in the household will be providing plenty of love and snuggles.

Another point to ponder, and one that can potentially lead to future problems—who's paying for what? If everyone's in agreement as to their financial obligations, great. If not, discuss, discuss, discuss! Leave some wiggle room for life's "what-if's" but try to strategize whenever possible. Remember that old saying, "It wasn't raining when Noah built the ark."

If there are children in your household, depending upon their age and physical limitations, this is a good opportunity to address obligations, time constraints, and schedules. For the safety of your children (and the dog) please don't expect a very young child to be capable of walking your new pet on a leash, picking up after it, or even spending time playing with it when not supervised by an adult. Someone can get hurt. A child who plays roughly can unintentionally injure a young puppy as well as an older dog. A puppy who's in the midst of teething and play-biting can likewise hurt your child.

Only you can judge the maturity of your child, but please be realistic when doling out responsibilities. It's up to you to teach everyone what's expected and what's acceptable or not. Ensure that the rules and limitations are very clear—including respect for kids' AND dog's personal space as well as their possessions. Dogs and children both need to understand their boundaries. There are many "how-to" books and videos geared toward children of all ages. Reading really IS fundamental, and even more so when it comes to teaching them how their new dog will become a well-loved and well-behaved member of the family. Snuggle up on the couch with the kids with some hot chocolate and a good book that explains in simple terms everything they need to know about dog care and training their new furry best friend.

Introducing Your New Pet to Other Pets in the Home

In a perfect world, everyone gets along, including pets. In the real world, not so much. This is where a little planning can go a long way toward raising a respectful, lovable canine companion. We always hope for the best possible situation—the kind you see on those cute YouTube videos: cats snuggling with dogs, Chihuahuas and Great Danes romping together in a meadow of flowers. And if you're lucky enough to have that rare combination of animal admiration and affection, it's a wonderful thing.

But let's not leave it to luck. Let's do some strategizing ahead of time and get things off on the right foot, or...paw. As a dog trainer, I would always use this example: Imagine you're in a loving, secure home, with a partner (spouse, etc.) who means the world to you. One day, that love of your life breezes in, just in time for dinner, announces, "Honey, I'm home, and I have a surprise! Look who's coming to live with us!" And in walks a young, handsome/beautiful stranger, who parks themselves at the dining room table, eats your food, watches your TV, and generally makes themselves at home. Forever. That's how it can feel to your already-established-in-the-household pet when the newcomer arrives.

Even if your dog or cat (or other species of pet) is the welcoming kind, do your best to prepare everyone ahead of time. If possible, obtain an item or toy that has your new Airedale's scent, bring it into the home, and let everyone check it out to become familiar with that "new dog smell." When you're ready to introduce your Airedale to another dog in the home, do it on neutral turf—a park, or somewhere your dog doesn't consider his own territory, and enlist the help of another person. Have both animals on leash, let the dogs meet and greet, get acquainted the way dogs love to do, and keep to an upbeat, friendly atmosphere. When it's time to bring them into the home, unless you're sure they will be at least cordial to one another, let them stay in separate rooms, with their own beds, food and water, and toys. A baby gate between rooms works well. That way, they can see, smell, and check each other out without any potentially problematic contact. At some point, there may be some stress, jealousy, or resentment, so pay equal attention to everyone.

When bringing a new dog into a home where there's a cat, make your cat's safety a priority. Keep her litter box, food, and water away from your dog, in a separate and secure area where the dog cannot invade her space. Keep the dog leashed, so she cannot frighten the cat (or the cat cannot scare the dog, depending upon your cat's personality). If they seem agree-

CHAPTER 4   Preparing for Your New Arrival

Photo Courtesy of Robin Peterson

able to meeting up close and personal, let them sniff each other while the dog remains on leash. Try placing a baby gate between rooms. It may take some time, but more often than not cats and dogs will eventually get along just fine in the same home. My own menagerie these days is composed of two cats and a dog. They all tolerate each other. They don't especially like each other, but they've managed to work out a somewhat peaceful existence. Every now and then if the dog gets too up close and personal, she'll get whacked in the head by a cat claw, but for the most part, everyone gets along, and there's some semblance of peace on earth, goodwill toward other pets. I've come to accept that we'll never witness an interspecies love-fest in our home, but there's no bloodshed either.

We always hope that in the long run, everyone will be happy, and with a dash of commitment, a cup of preparation, and maybe a spoonful of prayers, you'll have all the ingredients for a harmonious household recipe.

CHAPTER 5
Hidden Household Dangers

"Puppy Proof everything!!! Be aware that a 4 or 5 month old Airedale is tall enough to reach up on counters and tables, so make sure you have things put away so they can't get to them."

Anne Ramseyer
Annes Airedales LLC

Photo Courtesy of Luke Slater

Airedale Terriers, no matter how young or old, are notorious for trying to outsmart even the most conscientious dog owner. They're an intelligent, curious breed of dog, and they are like little stealth missiles when it comes to seeking out trouble. It is incumbent upon you, their owner/parent, to stay one step ahead of them AT ALL TIMES. Their safety should be a priority. Just look around and if you think there's even the slightest chance that something could create an unsafe situation for your dog, remove the temptation at all costs. Get down to their level. Do some crawling around. Is there an electrical cord that your dog can reach? Did a Lego block find its way under the sofa? Did one of the kids leave a dirty sock rolled up and stashed behind the recliner? You may be the best housekeeper in the world, but your dog will be seeing things from a whole different angle, and those things could be dangerous. Here's our short list of potential problems:

CHAPTER 5   Hidden Household Dangers

Crates

Yes, we know—what could possibly be unsafe about a crate? They're made for dogs, right? So they must be OK. Well, yes and no. Did we mention the time that Murphy the Airedale was determined to escape from her crate and got her head stuck between the door and the enclosure? If you're crate-training your pup, be sure your dog cannot manage to get any parts of her body wedged. If your dog wears a collar in the home, remove it before he goes into the crate.

Plants

Whether a plant is considered toxic or not, it's highly recommended that you remove ALL houseplants in reach of your new Airedale. Even if the plant is not known to be poisonous, the average curious dog will sniff out the dirt it's planted in, and dig, dig, dig. It may cause nothing more than a minor belly ache, or it may pose a more severe risk. Have you fertilized the soil in which your plant is growing? Have you used an insect repellent? Best to be safe and remove the temptation.

Photo Courtesy of Susannah Bell

The list of toxic plants is long, and includes both indoor and outdoor hazards. Some common indoor poisonous plants include dracaenas, calla lilies, jade plants, poinsettias, scheffleras, sansevierias, philodendrons, and aloe. Outside of your home, be on the lookout for holly, foxglove, vinca, azaleas, lilies of the valley, geraniums, boxwood, carnations, daffodils, boxwood, tulips, and begonias. One excellent source of reference is the ASPCA's list of Toxic and Non-Toxic Plants (ASPCA.org).

If you reside in a state where marijuana is legal, or if you or anyone in your household uses it for medicinal purposes, it's important to note that this substance, depending upon the amount ingested by a dog, can be deadly, so by all means, be sure to keep it away from your Airedale! There is ongoing research as to whether or not medically prescribed doses as well as oils made from the marijuana plant will benefit a dog in the case of some illnesses and conditions, but we urge you to consult with your veterinarian and not risk your dog's life by trying any substances without professional advice. In the event of an emergency, contact your local pet poison control center.

Toys

Photo Courtesy of Jeannine Mikowski

Airedales love to seek out and destroy stuffed toys, especially those with squeakers. A mischievous canine can rip the fluffy innards from a soft, cuddly dog toy quicker than you can say, "Drop it!" Children's toys with small parts, plastic board pieces, and dolls are all fair game for an Airedale. Rawhide bones can be hazardous and have the potential to cause a choking risk to a dog of any size or age. Needless to say, bones should be avoided, especially small ones and those which will splinter easily such as chicken bones. Even large marrow bones and rubbery bones manufactured especially for dogs can get stuck in a dog's mouth and block their airway.

My Airedale was fond of chasing tennis balls. Ever see what a cute pup can do to the fleecy outside of a tennis ball? Ever see what enough of that fleecy material can do to a puppy's stomach? Cords from window blinds and curtains should never be within your dog's reach. Caution: Airedales consider EVERYTHING edible—shoes, socks, wood, paper, metal and plastic objects, elastics, blankets, jewelry, pillows, anything leather—you get the idea. Puppies, especially, do not discriminate when it comes to what goes into their mouths. Keep a watchful eye!

Household chemicals

Including insecticides, rodent poisons, detergent, and cleaning agents. Airedales have been known to learn to open cabinet doors. What's under your sink? Baby safety locks are an inexpensive and effective investment to dog-proof your home.

CHAPTER 5   Hidden Household Dangers

Foods

Chocolate, raisins, grapes, nuts, garlic, onions, anything containing xylitol (in chewing gum and other substances), alcohol. Watch for reactions to any food your dog consumes. My own dog is allergic to pork and anything containing pork products. No bacon for you, sunshine!

In addition to those items already mentioned, products used on humans should not be used on your Airedale Terrier. Toothpaste, shampoos (even baby shampoo), soaps, vinegar, skin care products, mouthwash. The use of various essential oils has seen a rise in popularity, both in aromatherapy as well as topical application, but some oils can be irritating at best, toxic to dogs at worst. Tree tea oil, cinnamon, and citrus oils should not be used. However others such as lavender, lemongrass, and thyme may be utilized in small specified amounts.

Also, stay up to date on product recalls. No matter how organic or expensive the food you're feeding your dog may be, recalls are announced fairly often. Whenever you may be in doubt, consult with your veterinarian.

Photo Courtesy of Ruth Antoniuk

CHAPTER 6
Supplies for Your Dog

There are some essentials for your dog that are, well, essential. Before you bring home the newest member of your family, be sure to have on hand everything you'll need.

Crate

To crate or not to crate, that is the question. (OK, so Shakespeare may not have been referring to Airedale Terriers when he came up with his legendary inquiry, but nevertheless, it still deserves an answer.) I've done it both ways with my long history of doggy do's and don'ts, and I am wholeheartedly, 100%, absolutely and positively in favor of the crate. (Do we get the idea that I endorse using a crate?) Here's why:

CHAPTER 6   Supplies for Your Dog

We all need our own "space." Your husband needs (or wants) a man-cave. Sheila needs her "she shed." Your dog needs a crate. It's his bedroom, his chill-out space, his safe place. As long as you create a positive association with the crate, it will be his "go-to" spot to sleep, relax, play with his favorite stuffed toy, eat a nice treat, and get away from the neighbor's noisy kids who've just invaded the family room. If used properly, and not solely as a means of punishment or for long periods of time, the crate is your friend. And your dog's. It's also quite beneficial to a successful housetraining experience for your dog, and will keep him from selecting your oriental rug as his choice of bathroom location.

You can also have multiple crates, which is something I've chosen to do with my dogs. One crate is placed an area where she can just hang out with a toy or a treat, or to take a nap if she's tired during the day, or just to get away from the household activity. The other crate is next to my bed for night time sleeping. When your dog gets older and you can trust her to sleep through the night, with no accidents, you can allow her some freedom and if she (and you) prefer, take the crate away and allow her to sleep in her own bed. If she absolutely loves her crate, keep it. Consistency: just refer to her crate with the same word: box, kennel, crate, nest, room, space. Use a quiet voice, point, and say, "Time to go in your crate" (or whatever special word you're using). She'll soon grasp the idea. And you'll get the peace of mind that she's safe, secure, and has a place to call her own.

Size-wise, get a crate that will be large enough for your dog at any age. For an Airedale, a metal crate of approximately 48" by 30" is recommended. Heavy-duty plastic crates are also an option. Some crates come with dividers so that your dog can enjoy a smaller, cozier space when he's young, but can easily be removed as he grows and needs a bit more room.

Food

Check with the breeder, shelter, or foster home/rescue that your Airedale has called home most recently. They will advise you on the type and brand of food, as well as the amount, that your dog should be eating. Do not change his diet. Your dog will be experiencing enough adjustments in the coming days and weeks, so unless otherwise recommended by your veterinarian or your pet's previous caregivers, continue feeding him whatever he is used to. If you plan to make changes, this is not the time. Consult with your vet on future feeding recommendations, and discuss any dietary, health, and/or cost concerns that you may have.

Food and water bowls

Metal and ceramic bowls are widely recommended. Plastic bowls are also available, but these can sometimes look like a chewy toy to your dog.

Leashes and harnesses

Most dog obedience trainers will recommend a 6-foot-long leather leash. They may cost a bit more, but will be easier on your hands. The other good news is that this type of leash can last a long, long time. I have a leather leash that I've been using for at least 15 years, and although it started off quite stiff, as most leathers do, it's nicely broken in, soft and pliable, and I will likely have it for another 15 years. Nylon and cotton leashes can fray and irritate hands, and although you might be tempted by the outstanding selection of colors and designs, my advice is to go with the leather. (Be sure to keep the leash out of your dog's mouth when on walks, and let it be known to your dog that his leash is not a toy.)

Retractable leashes should not be an option with a new dog, young or old, so please put that on the back burner until you are sure your dog is well trained, responsive to commands, and doesn't pull. Using a leash of this type can be a definite safety issue, so consider your Airedale's well-being if you're thinking about purchasing a retractable leash. Your dog needs to be at your side, at least for now. Harnesses are another option that you'll find recommended by some, abhorred by others. I have personally found that a dog on a harness tends to be less responsive to me, but in some cases, a harness might be the preferred option. When teaching a dog to walk on a leash, I most definitely prefer a collar; however, for more casual activities such as hiking, a harness can be the appropriate choice.

If you opt for a collar instead of a harness, be sure to see that it fits snugly enough so that your dog cannot pull his head out from the collar. This is something I do EVERY time I put the collar on my dog. If your dog is out in the rain, swimming, or just playing, all collars have a tendency to stretch a bit. You may not realize it on a day-to-day basis, but it's always a good idea to check and make adjustments when needed. With a growing dog, check often for a too-tight fit.

For an older dog with mobility issues or painful joints, a harness can provide support and assistance in standing or walking. Mobility issues also affect people, as we're all aware, and for those who have bad backs and problems bending, a harness may be difficult to maneuver when it comes to getting it on and off your dog. A nylon collar could possibly cause injury to a dog's trachea, thyroid, or ears on a dog who has yet to learn the concept of "no pull."

You can see that there are positives and negatives to collars and harnesses, but the choice ultimately must depend upon the age, behavior, and health of each individual dog. It's to everyone's advantage to work with a trainer who can determine whether your dog's temperament, responsiveness to commands, and physical needs are best suited to a collar or harness. If you have a preference or reason for using one over another, discuss it with the trainer in advance.

Identification tags

No dog should be without an ID. Even if you haven't decided on a name for your Airedale yet, get to a pet store or online vendor ASAP and have an identification tag imprinted. I prefer NOT to put my dog's name on the tag, and simply state, "If found, please call 781-555-5555." Again, it's a personal decision. Additionally, your dog should have his rabies tag as well as the town's dog license number tag on his collar or harness. My dog wears her microchip tag as well. There's plenty of contact information if your pet is found wandering. If you prefer not to listen to metal tags jingling whenever your dog walks by, an easy solution is to wrap a small piece of Velcro around all of the tags. Voila! No more noise!

Dog bed

Yes, your dog needs her own bed, her safe place, her space. If you're crate-training your dog, you can put her bed in the crate, and when and if she no longer needs the crate, you can move her bed elsewhere. As with so many other recommendations, there are pros and cons to having a dog sleep in her human's bed. I am wholeheartedly against the idea, but it's a very personal decision. My reasons? I've seen too many dogs with aggression issues, and in many of those cases, it centers around the bed. It's a chicken or egg situation. Did being on the bed create the aggression or was the aggression there first? Cause/effect, no one knows.

Yes, it's cuddly, warm, and in some cultures, preferable and totally acceptable to sleep with your pet, but here are a few things to consider: Is your dog outside during the day, walking on dirt and asphalt, just like you? Is there a reason you remove your shoes before going to bed at night? Your dog can't, so count on the dirt and germs to accompany her into your bed. Do you like a good night's sleep without getting poked and prodded by not two but four legs? What if you've got a dog who considers your bed his personal domain, and when you reprimand him, he responds by urinating on the mattress? It happens more frequently than most would care to admit, but dog trainers see it all too often. The owner will then have the additional issue of keeping the dog OFF the bed. Not an easy task. So my question would be, why start? I have always compromised and kept the dog bed in my bedroom, NEXT to my bed. Everyone's happy, and we get a decent night's sleep.

What Kind of Dog Bed? So many beds, so little time…What's the best type of bed for your dog? Have you ever gone into a mattress store and felt thoroughly overwhelmed with the number of selections? Start off with size. Big dog = big bed. Likewise, small dog = small bed. (If you're awaiting the arrival of a puppy, remember that your dog will grow quickly and will soon need a bigger bed.) Next, consider bolster type, flat, fluffy, firm, Memory Foam, round, square, rectangular.

If your dog is older with joint soreness or limited mobility, there are also off-the-floor cot-style beds as well as orthopedic beds. For warmer or cooler climates, there are heated and cooled beds. If you will be crate-training your dog, get a bed that will fit in the crate. Will your dog's sleep mode be the sprawled out version, or will she curl up fetal-style? If your dog is still with the breeder or in a foster home, add to your list of questions: How does my dog like to sleep? This can give you some guidance when purchasing a bed.

Coat/Paw Protection

Little and big paws alike can be especially sensitive to the elements, as well as sand, salt, and ice melt products. Although it may be a bit of a struggle to get your Airedale used to wearing them, consider boots for your dog if you live in a cold climate. Whether you live in snowy Wisconsin or sunny Florida, it's a good idea to purchase a jar of paw wax. Not only will it protect your dog's feet from ice, salt, and snow during winter months, but also from sand and hot sidewalks in the summer. It moisturizes paws as well, so it's less likely your dog will suffer from cracked pads.

For those of us who must grin and bear the cold winter weather, we suggest you invest in a coat for your dog. Airedales are hardy souls, but especially for a young pup or a senior dog, a coat will be most welcome, and you'll be surprised at the amount of heat you'll feel from inside the coat when you remove it. Water-repellant coats are also great for rainy days. We prefer a vest-like coat, with Velcro enclosures rather than full jackets. It's just easier to get on and off, but if you'd prefer something a little fancier, there are plenty of styles from which to choose. Lately I've noticed that some of the dogs in my neighborhood are dressed better than I am. Not sure if that's a good thing.

CHAPTER 6   Supplies for Your Dog

Toys

"Provide toys and entertainment. A bored Airedale is a destructive Airedale!"

Anne Ramseyer
Annes Airedales LLC

The first consideration when choosing any toy for your dog should be safety. If your dog tends to disembowel every toy you give him, you'll be at the pet store on a daily basis replenishing the supply to keep him occupied. If you're handy (lucky you!), making your own toys is always an option. In either case, your dog will need a variety of "friends" to hang out with. Kong toys (or similar brands) which can be filled with small treats are highly recommended once your dog is able to easily digest the treats. Balls that squeak are always a favorite pastime, and many Airedales can't resist a fleecy stuffed companion. Chewy rubber-like toys are loved by most dogs. There's no end to the variety, and every dog will have his or her favorite.

For a young dog, I've found that wetting a heavy sock or wash cloth with water, wringing it out, and placing it in the freezer for a few hours will give plenty of comfort and fun to a teething dog's sore mouth. Another do-it-yourself toy (again, the old sock trick) is to stuff an empty plastic water bottle minus the cap into a tube sock, tie off both ends, and let your Airedale

Photo Courtesy of Carly Kanipe

Photo Courtesy of Madeleine Horn
Bred by DogwoodDales of Sherman, Texas

enjoy the "crunchy" texture and noise. Tug of war type toys should be introduced with a word of caution: if your dog shows any aggressive tendencies, these should be avoided. Unless your dog understands "drop it" and can play tug of war on your terms (i.e., letting go when you ask her to), find a better alternative. Rawhide, sticks, and any toy that can be swallowed easily are definite no-nos. Safety first, and keep a watchful eye at all times.

Poop bags/bag holders

You can get fancy here or not. We choose the latter. Spending more money than is necessary on poop bags just doesn't fit our style. Our local supermarket sells a box of 75 clear plastic bags with ties for about $1.50. When duty calls, we slide our hand in a bag, scoop up the poop, turn it inside out, and tie it in a knot to close it off. (No need to use the more expensive and not-so-practical "slide enclosure" bags. We keep a small covered trash can in the garage to dispose of the bags until trash day. Easy-peasy. You can purchase special poop bags online or at pet stores, but the no-name storage size bags work just as well and are much cheaper. We don't particularly care if they're green or pink, or have little paw prints stamped on them. The dog doesn't really seem to mind, either.

One of the best investments in our vast array of doggy equipment has been a small rubber poop bag holder that attaches to the handle of your leash. For a whopping $4.95 (online or in most pet stores) your hands are free to hold the leash, your pockets don't smell like "essence of dog droppings" when you hang up your coat in the closet and forget the bag is still in there from the day before, and you've got a free hand to wave to the neighbors or give your Airedale a head pat.

Treats

Small training treats will help make your dog respond nicely. It's so much easier to get your dog to pay attention to you when you've got a pocket full of yummy goodies. Lots of praise works nicely, but reinforcing good behavior with a little something extra for your chow hound is an added bonus for both you and your dog. Treats should be of the bite-sized variety. Check with your vet to see if there is a preferred brand.

Odor Neutralizer

This is an item where it's best to buy a high-quality product that's especially made to remove dog urine and feces stains and odors. If your new dog has an accident (and more likely than not, she will) removing the odor in a timely and effective manner will discourage her from using that same spot in the future. Do not use ammonia- or vinegar-based products, which can imitate the smell of your dog's urine and encourage her to use that spot again. There are many good brands available, so have plenty on hand, just in case.

Grannick's Bitter Apple Spray

This product has saved many a wonderful dog/human relationship, not to mention furniture and fabrics. Keep a bottle handy to spray anything your dog shows an interest in that you'd prefer he didn't. We've used it on sofa legs, carpet edges, decorative pillows, you name it. You can even use it on your dog if at any time he develops hot spots (check with your vet first, please). If your dog is obsessed with chewing his leash, this may deter him, so apply some Bitter Apple directly on the leash. It's non-toxic, usually sells for less than $6 per bottle, and you won't smell it, but your dog will. Of course, there's always a chance that you've got that one dog who won't really care that it tastes bad, but in most cases, it's definitely worth trying. It's advisable to spray a small amount first on items, to be sure there won't be any damage or fabric discoloration, but we've never found this to be the case in many, many years of using it.

Grooming Supplies

"We recommend our owners brush regularly with Mars Coat King or similar stripping comb. And be sure not to over bathe your Airedale!"

Tony Hogg
North FL Airedales

As early as feasibly possible, get your dog used to a grooming routine. Whether you plan to groom him yourself or choose to bring your dog to a professional groomer, it should be done on a regular basis. At least once a week, preferably twice, brush your dog with a slicker brush or wire brush with soft "pin" tips. Some Airedales have sensitive skin, so be gentle. Your Airedale's beard will be a dirt magnet. Be prepared to keep it clean, especially after feeding. (A wet washcloth works well.) Airedales drip. Get used to it. Ears must also be cleaned frequently (no cotton swabs, please! A soft cloth or cotton ball is recommended here).

Teeth brushing should also be part of your dog's good grooming routine, and while you can use a soft brush made for humans, there are specially designed brushes for our canine companions. However, do NOT use toothpaste made for humans. Fluoride and other chemicals in the toothpaste can be hazardous. Brushing your dog's teeth on a daily basis is ideal, but several times a week is a good hygiene habit for your dog.

If you need to bathe and shampoo your dog, do it no more than once every few months. Airedales are prone to dry skin, and frequent shampooing can remove moisture and oils. Not a good thing. If you DO need to bathe your dog, be sure to brush and comb him out before bathing, to remove any loose hair. Otherwise, you may need to keep a good drain cleaning service on speed dial. Use a shampoo that's made specifically for your dog's type of coat, and never, ever use shampoo or any soap made for humans.

Most of the Airedale grooming process is fairly routine and easily learned, but "some of us" will readily admit to being squeamish when it comes to clipping a dog's nails. If you have any hesitation whatsoever about this, allow your groomer or veterinarian to do the honors. I can do most anything that I set my mind to. Except trim a dog's nails.

CHAPTER 6   Supplies for Your Dog

Dog car seats, harnesses, tethers, restraints

What dog doesn't love going for a ride in the car? Well, okay, there's always one. But if you're hopeful that your new Airedale will be a great car companion, you'll need to consider your options. Where and how will she ride? There is a wide variety of restraints, from the simplest seat belt adapter, to pricey car seats, and everything in between. A few states require dogs to be harnessed or seat belted when riding in a vehicle, and other states are in the process of taking this under advisement, so it is important to adhere to your state's laws. For the safety of your pet, and for your own safety, do not allow your dog to ride "shotgun" in the front seat of your car. A sudden stop could be deadly to your pet. And please, please, please, don't let your dog sit on your lap while you're driving. It's just plain dangerous.

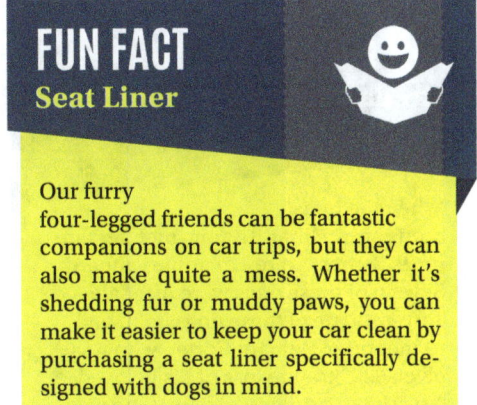

FUN FACT
Seat Liner

Our furry four-legged friends can be fantastic companions on car trips, but they can also make quite a mess. Whether it's shedding fur or muddy paws, you can make it easier to keep your car clean by purchasing a seat liner specifically designed with dogs in mind.

Fencing, dog gates

If you are fortunate enough to have an enclosed yard, the fence height must be high enough to keep your dog from jumping over. You would be very surprised at the height a springy-legged Airedale can attain when they are so inclined. A 5- or 6-foot fence is preferable. Don't overlook the concept of locking your gate, if possible. A friendly dog, outside alone, can be enticed by anyone desiring an adorable Airedale. Your letter carrier or delivery person may inadvertently leave the gate door open. Suddenly, you're missing your beloved dog, so don't take a chance. Electronic fences are another option, but professional installation is recommended, and your dog MUST also be professionally trained as to respecting boundaries.

Dog gates, baby gates, and dog play pens are great to have in the home, and will give your Airedale sufficient room to explore. All gates should be secured correctly. It's easy to put your pup in a small room, thinking it will keep her out of harm's way, but that's not always the case. Sad (and costly) example: A neighbor had a dog who was afraid of thunderstorms. As he had to be away for an hour or two, he put his dog in a good-sized bathroom, with plenty of toys to keep him amused. Cue the thunderstorm. The dog was terrified, and managed to chew his way through some plumbing. The owner returned to find his dog very scared, his bathroom very wet, and his home very flooded.

Emergency kit

FUN FACT
Airedales on the Titanic

When the infamous ocean liner, Titanic, met her fate in 1912, there were 12 canines aboard. Several of these dogs were Airedale Terriers. One of these dogs belonged to the son of William Carter, who was given $200 for the loss of his beloved pet. The two other Airedales who went down with this ship belonged to John Jacob Astor IV and his wife.

Accidents, disasters, and unforeseen situations happen without warning. It's a good idea to put together an emergency preparedness kit for your beloved pet. Include: a list (and phone numbers) of local hotels who will accept dogs (check in advance), a leash and/or harness, blankets, a first aid kit, a pet carrier, food, bottled water, food/water bowls, a few toys, a copy of your dog's up-to-date health records with the name and contact information for her veterinarian, and any medications your pet needs. Be sure she is wearing her collar with identification tags. Keep a photo of your dog on your phone or in a handy location. If, for some reason, you and your pet become separated, you will be able to make copies of the photo to circulate online or on posters.

Location, Location, Location

You're almost ready. Your dog is waiting to come to her new home. You've got the supplies you'll need. Everyone knows what their responsibilities will be, and are eagerly awaiting the new arrival. Not so fast. Let's just take a moment to figure out the logistics. Your dog will need space. Someplace calm, comfortable, and out of the way. If you're using a crate, that's the perfect place for your dog to have some privacy when she just needs to chill. Locate it in a quiet corner of your home, away from the daily hustle and bustle. Some dogs prefer to still see what's going on around them, while others need to be off on their own. If you're not using a crate, then the dog bed is the next best thing. In my house, we've got a dog bed in the kitchen, one in the bedroom, and one in the family room. Besides a dog, they usually contain some fleecy toys, a small blanket, and whatever else our pup decides she absolutely needs to have handy. The one thing those beds have in common is that they are all tucked away, either in a corner or against a wall or other furniture. She can always retreat to her space, take a snooze, or keep watch on the comings and goings of the family. But wherever she chooses to crash, she always feels safe and secure.

We have several toy boxes in various locations for our dog, so that when she's in the mood to play, she knows where her belongings are located. It makes clean-up easy, and everything stays where she can find it. You can purchase a specially designed dog toy box, or use a heavy cardboard or plastic bin. Check often for signs of wear and tear. We had a dog visitor once who decided that the toy box was a lot more interesting than the toys that were contained therein. We invested in a sturdier model.

We keep our leashes hanging on pegs in the mud room, so they're always nearby for a walk. We also keep an extra leash in every car, in case of emergency. (On several occasions, we've had to use that extra leash to rescue other people's wandering dogs.) Depending on who is dropping off or picking up the dog at our friendly neighborhood doggy day care facility, there's always a leash ready for dog transportation.

Before your dog comes to her new home, it's a good idea to decide where her food and water bowls will be located. Dogs are pack animals, and they love eating with their pack—that's you and your family. The kitchen is a great spot, but if possible, try to place your pet's food and water bowls in an area that receives little foot traffic. It's definitely preferable not to have everyone stepping over a bowl of dog food, and if your dog is at all anxious about her new surroundings, she'll like it much better if she has a little privacy when eating. Airedales can be a bit sloppy around food and water. An inexpensive plastic placemat under their bowls will help to protect your floors.

What's in a Name?

People seem to be much more creative these days when it comes to naming their dogs. That's a good thing. Not so very long ago, we had Duke (and his lady, Duchess), Princess and her Prince, Lassie, Spot, Lucky, Rex. In my neighborhood alone, we had several dogs named Buddy, two who answered to Tippy, and a couple of Fluffys. If your new dog is coming to your home from a shelter, the nice folks who lovingly looked after your future Airedale gave him a name, however temporary. (If they were familiar with his previous owners and history, it would have been his original name.) If that's the case, then keeping his name is a good idea. New owners, new home, new surroundings—at this point, he doesn't need to get used to a new name as well. Unless, of course, that name just doesn't do it for you. If you must change it, try something that sounds similar. Bella could be Stella. Bailey could become Hailey. Harley could be Marley. A pocket full of treats and lots of praise will work wonders to help your dog to learn his new name. Try a simple command using his new name, followed by a treat and some enthusiastic praise. "Bubba, come." And when Bubba arrives for his treat, "Good Bubba! What a good boy!" Always use his name for good things. Keep his name out of any negative comments, as in, "Bad Bubba!" Let Bubba associate his new name with everything wonderful in his world.

If you've got a puppy arriving, the name game is a little less complicated. Decide well in advance on the ideal name for your new pet. If he's coming from a breeder, let them know so they can begin using his name. What to call him? Here are a few helpful hints: One- or two-syllable names work best. Any more than that, and chances are pretty good it will be shortened eventually. You may be a student of Greek mythology, but you might want

CHAPTER 6   Supplies for Your Dog

to reconsider "Aphrodite" as a potential name for your dog. I love everything Les Miserables, but somehow "Murphy" was a bit more appropriate than Jean Valjean as a name for my Airedale. Be creative, be original, but keep it simple.

Some dog trainers have a theory that your dog will tend to "live up to" his name. Picture this scenario: You meet another dog owner and their pet at the dog park. "What's your dog's name?" you inquire. "Killer," he replies. The odds are you'll gather up your dog and walk quickly in the opposite direction. Let's try that again. "What's your dog's name?" "His name is Happy." Okay, then, let's play! Just something to be mindful of when choosing the best name for your best friend.

CHAPTER 7
Welcoming Your Airedale to His New Home

Timing is everything. Bring your new dog home when you and your household members can give him your undivided attention for as long as possible. If you can, plan on an early weekend arrival home. If you've got company staying over, weekend activities, if you're preoccupied with holiday preparations, it's best to delay his arrival until things are quiet and you can focus on getting your dog acclimated to his new environment.

The Ride Home

Pack ahead of time for the ride. Even if you're only traveling a short distance, take along poop bags, some paper towels, your dog's new leash and collar (be sure he can't slip his head out of the collar if you need to stop at a rest area for a bathroom break), a toy or two, some treats, and, depending upon the weather, a small blanket in which to wrap him. If he's coming from his breeder, try to bring home a toy or some fabric that has his mama's scent on it. He'll be missing her.

This may be your Airedale's first time in a car. You'll want it to be an enjoyable experience for everyone, especially your new dog, as it will set the stage for future car rides. This is where an extra set of hands (or an additional warm lap and calm demeanor) will most certainly be beneficial. If you're opting for a car harness, start with his first ride home. Your new dog should travel on a reasonably empty stomach, and be certain that he's had a chance to move his bowels and urinate before the trip home. If you're traveling a long distance, take some bathroom breaks along the way, and if needed, some food, water and bowls for a longer trip. Some small treats can make the trip pleasant. If you do need to stop, your puppy should not be allowed near other dogs or go in an area where other dogs have relieved themselves. Most veterinarians recommend that a pup be kept away from unknown dogs and places where they've been until after your dog has received his vaccinations. Don't put your puppy's health at risk for any canine communicable diseases.

CHAPTER 7 Welcoming Your Airedale to His New Home

Photo Courtesy of Daniel Morgan

First Night in His New Home

Imagine what it's like to be a puppy. You've spent your entire life in your nice, warm home, with your mama, had a meal and snacks whenever your little tummy started to rumble, played with lots of soft toys, and your siblings were always there to snuggle. Life was good. Or maybe you're an older dog who hasn't had such a great life, but you were just getting used to the sights and sounds of the animal shelter. You no longer had to forage for food, it was warm, and there were nice people around to take you for a walk or scratch your head. Now, all of a sudden, you're in a strange place, with unfamiliar people and sounds, and all sorts of weird new sights and smells. Heck, they're not even calling you by your real name. What's going on? What's happening? Mommy, I'm scared!

This is the time to put some good old-fashioned R 'n' R into action. No, not Rock and Roll. No, not Rest and Recreation. The R 'n' R we're referring to here is Reassurance and Routine. Let your dog get used to her new surroundings in her own way. Don't give her too much space at first. Block off a room for her, where she can feel comfortable. Don't overwhelm her with too much stimulation. The neighborhood kids may already be knocking on the front door to check out the adorable new puppy or the dog you've just adopted, but it's in everyone's best interest to delay the meet and greet until things have settled down a bit. Your new furry kid needs time to adjust, to relax, and to explore her new digs. She may be tired, she may be fearful, or she may be eager to play. Every dog will react differently, but it's up to you to keep things calm. There will be plenty of time for adventures soon. Sit with your dog, speak in a quiet, upbeat voice, let her know that all is right in this, her new world.

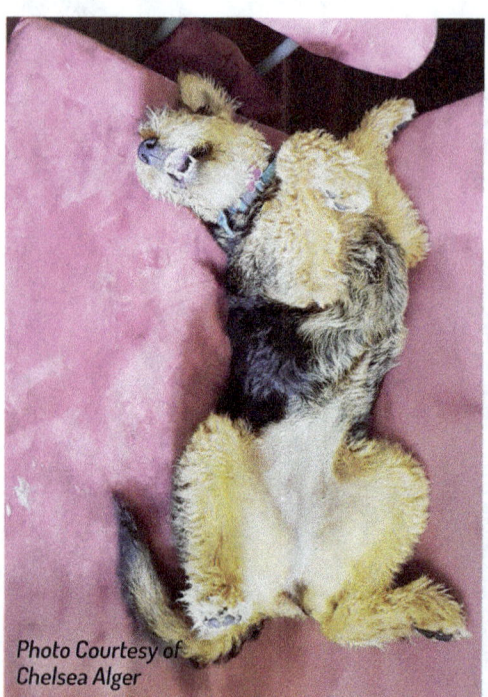
Photo Courtesy of Chelsea Alger

The second "R" is Routine, and that's equally as important as Reassurance. Get your dog acquainted with her new schedule quickly. Take

CHAPTER 7 Welcoming Your Airedale to His New Home

her out for bathroom breaks as soon as she eats or drinks, and take her to the same location each and every time. Praise her to the moon and back whenever she does something good. Let her think that peeing in the back yard next to the big maple tree is the best thing that's ever happened in the history of the world. Reward her with a small treat. Did we mention praise? You can't say, "What a good girl!" enough. On the other hand, there are bound to be accidents, and when there are, there's no need to yell. A loud, angry voice will only frighten an already anxious dog. Remember that old saying about "catching more flies with honey"? You can get your point across just as well with a mildly disappointed tone to your voice. Remember, it's up to you to TEACH your dog what's expected of her.

> **FUN FACT**
> **Airedales in the White House**
>
> Records held by the Presidential Pet Museum show that three Airedale terriers have been White House pets. The first Airedale terrier to take up residence at the White House was Davie, owned by President Woodrow Wilson, followed by Laddie Boy, pet to President Warren Harding. Most recently, President Calvin Coolidge had an Airedale named Paul Pry.

If you've adopted a new dog, there's just as much of a learning curve—for both of you—as with a young puppy. Even though you might think he's housetrained, he may "forget" in the excitement of being in a new home. Be patient. He's stressed, nervous, and unsure of what to do. He may have been in an abusive or neglectful situation and may not react as you'd expect. He needs time to adjust, so be patient. On the other hand, you may have adopted a dog who settles in so nicely to his new home that everyone is just in awe at how well he's adapting. You may have found that perfect dog!

Or…you may be enjoying what dog trainers often refer to as "the honeymoon phase." Among the many outstanding qualities that Airedale Terriers possess is an amazing amount of intelligence and the ability to use their instincts to analyze any given situation. So your new dog may be thinking, "Well, OK, they seem nice enough. I'll just hang out here for a while, be on my best behavior until I figure out who's in charge, and then, it's all about me." It usually takes about 2 weeks on average for the honeymoon phase to come to a screeching halt. Your new dog is now very much at home, and the testing will most likely commence. However, if you've prepared in advance, and can anticipate that it may happen, if and when it does, it can be a win-win situation. We'll explain more when we discuss training your Airedale.

Photo Courtesy of Brad Peas

CHAPTER 7   Welcoming Your Airedale to His New Home

Your dog's first night in his new home will be a challenging experience for everyone. You'll be listening for doggy sounds. Your dog will be listening for people sounds. A young puppy will surely be missing her litter mates and her mama, and everything that she's become familiar with up until now. You'll be missing a good night's sleep. Take comfort in knowing that this won't last too long, and your beauty rest will be forthcoming. But for now...

Let's get back to the routine (there's that "R" word again). Consistency is of utmost importance. If you've got a puppy, watch her for signs that she needs to relieve herself. You'll become familiar with these signals quite quickly. She may whimper, start to spin in a circle, or she may just squat and go. Every dog has his or her own way of doing things. Your breeder may have already begun the housetraining process. If that's the case, you're ahead of the game, so continue on the breeder's recommended schedule.

If you haven't determined yet whether crate training your dog is the route to take, housetraining may be the deciding factor. It usually makes the process much easier and quicker. Plus it will mean that your dog is less likely to relieve himself in random locations around your home. Trainers and veterinarians theorize that a dog who is approximately four months old and older should be able to hold their urine and feces equal to the approximate number of months they reach. A 4-month-old dog should be able to wait 4 hours. But there's an exception to every rule, and your dog may be it. At such a young age, their stomachs and bladders are small. Don't feed or give your dog food or water before bed. A 12-week-old pup should be taken out to relieve himself every 3 hours during the night. This time should be extended gradually to 3½, 4, then 4½ hours, etc., until he can make it through the night.

It's important to do a little preparation work ahead of time for your nightly outings.

Before going to bed, have everything ready that you'll need later: leash, collar, poop bags, flashlight, clothes, shoes. Anticipate weather conditions accordingly. If your dog is crying to go out, and it takes you an additional 20 minutes to find your sneakers, your pup may not be able to wait.

For everyone's peace of mind, understand that nighttime housetraining and daytime housetraining should be approached differently. During the day, you'll praise your dog, give him a treat, take him for a walk, reward him for being a star student in the potty training process. At night, you're not going to reinforce his good behavior with quite as many lavish rewards. Nighttime is business time, not playtime. Quietly put on his collar and leash, walk him outside to the same spot where you want him to go, keep him outside for no more than 10 or 15 minutes, and praise him with a quick, "good boy." No treats, no fun stuff for him to look forward to, just get out, do your thing, and back to bed. Thank you very much, now let's get some sleep.

Photo Courtesy of Val Allan

Always use the same phrases for him to associate with his potty habits. "Go do peeps," "Go do poops," whatever words you'd prefer to use. You can say "Peanut butter and jelly" if it works for you, but remain consistent. Everyone in the household who shares in the potty training responsibility should be using these same words. My 2 dogs learned their housetraining commands from an early age. People marveled when I said, "Go do peeps" and they both went at exactly the same time. Nothing like synchronized peeing to have the neighbors applauding your dog training skills. Remember: CONSISTENCY is KEY!

Don't assume that if you've adopted an older dog, the housetraining will be easier than with a young puppy. We ideally hope that it will be, but it can sometimes take even longer. Separation anxiety, a new home situation, unfamiliar routine, traumatic circumstances can all contribute to housetraining issues. Example: your new dog may have spent much of his life outside, and now he's in the house. How could he know where to go? Sometimes people in colder climates use newspapers or "pee pads" for their pets. Your dog now thinks, "OK, so NOW what am I supposed to do?" He may be marking his new territory, or may be a "submissive pee-er." Be sure that there are no medical conditions that could contribute to frequent urination, such as a bladder or kidney infection. (If you suspect that this may be the case, it's essential to consult with your veterinarian and obtain proper treatment.) An older dog can experience just as much stress, if not more, surrounding his housetraining experience.

If an accident happens in the house and you're not there to correct it, it does absolutely no good to reprimand him AFTER the fact. He will not be able to associate your displeasure with his housetraining mistake that happened an hour ago. Clean it immediately, neutralize the odor so that your dog won't be tempted to return to his chosen indoor bathroom spot, and the next time he's to be commended for good behavior, continue with your encouragement, praise, and rewards. Be patient, and be consistent.

There's a trick that I've used with my dogs to have them signal when they need to go out for a bathroom break: I simply hang a short ribbon with a bell from my front door knob, which they learned to ring when "it's time!" I start by ringing the bell myself when the dog gets near the door, and say, "Let's go out to pee/poop." Of course, a crafty Airedale may figure out that ringing the bell will also get him outside whenever he feels like socializing with the neighbor's dog, or wants to go for a walk around the block, so it is incumbent upon you to educate him to the rules of discriminating between going out for potty time and playtime. Otherwise you'll be hearing bells...a lot.

Congratulations! You're a Dog Parent!

Your Airedale has arrived. Adjustments are being made. Routines are being established, and you're confident that things are going along pretty well. And then they're not. The puppy is nipping at the kids. He's barking and keeping the baby from her naps. He's been chewing the chair legs and jumping on the furniture. Do any of these behaviors sound familiar? Take heart. It's not a totally bad thing, because it indicates that your dog is starting to feel more comfortable in his new home. On the other hand, all of the above mentioned behaviors are unacceptable. It's time to get this Airedale some training, formal or informal. Just recognize that the longer you, as his dog parent, wait, the more difficult it will be to alleviate the unwanted behavior. Procrastination is not your friend.

CHAPTER 8
Where Are Your Manners?

Some dogs are easier to train than others. They just "get it." For instance, I'm convinced that my little rescue dog, who came from down south in Georgia, was born an "old soul." She was 4 months old when we adopted her, never needed any formal training, responded to commands immediately, and walks perfectly both on and off leash.

My Airedale Murphy, however, spent an inordinate amount of time in dog obedience school. I've calculated that it was the equivalent of receiving her master's degree from Harvard—from the perspective of time as well as money. It wasn't because she was dumb. Quite the opposite. She was an Airedale—sweet, stubborn, and extremely smart. She was a champion at pushing our buttons and testing to see how far she could go before we'd notice her mischief du jour. I remember one particular day, when we arrived home to find her sitting on top of the dining room table with a banana in front of her. Said banana had previously been located on the kitchen counter, which we were certain was out of her reach. Upon further inspection, we noticed that the inside of the banana had been eaten, while the banana peel had been carefully put back in place, so we wouldn't notice the misdemeanor. Murphy was off to the dog trainer quicker than you can say, "We need help!"

Please don't assume that dog obedience trainers should be called in as a last resort. Far from it. Sooner, rather than later, is the best time to start training your dog. It's obvious that trainers specialize in training. But that doesn't necessarily mean their practices are limited to working with dogs with severe behavioral problems. Some trainers specialize in working with puppies, geriatric dogs, or dogs with special needs. Others specialize in working with families, basic commands, aggression issues, off-leash work, or dog socialization skills, to name but a few. A good, professional trainer is committed to working not ONLY with the dog, but with the dog's owner(s) and all members of the household as well.

FUN FACT
Airedale Terrier Club of America (ATCA)

The ATCA was founded in 1900 and is the official breed club for Airedales. This organization aims to maintain a breed standard and further the interests of the breed. To become a member, you must be at least 18 years old, be in good standing with the American Kennel Club (AKC), and adhere to the objectives of the ATCA. For more information about the club, visit www.Airedale.org.

Working on your own without a trainer is another option, but it's up to you to educate yourself on the best teaching methods, and understand how your dog responds. Some dogs need only a gentle suggestion, while others need a bit firmer approach. In any case, your ultimate goal is a well-mannered dog. And let us not limit your Airedale's training to commands. Just as every human needs mental stimulation, problem-solving challenges, and physical exercise, your new dog requires these things as well. But let's start with the commands for now.

Training Your Airedale Terrier

Dogs are pack animals. They travel with their pack, eat and sleep with their pack, play with their pack members. YOU are the leader of their pack now. Your dog looks to you for nourishment, guidance, affection, entertainment, security. Do not let him down. He will constantly question whether you are worthy of the title of "Top Dog" and will test (probably over and over again) to see if you're actually in charge. If he sees that there's a deficiency here, he'll be happy to step up to the plate and take over as Chief.

It's up to you to convince him that you are, indeed, Alpha Dog. In the canine world, Mother Dog does not yell, fight, cry, or lose control when one of her offspring becomes unruly. She is the authority figure, lets her displeasure be known with a quiet but very effective growl, and her young hooligan immediately realizes that he'd better shape up. If you want to earn your dog's respect, you'll need to become Mother Dog.

As a professional dog trainer, my favorite method of getting my point across to new dog parents boiled down to these two words: Benevolent Dictator. You are in charge, you are to be respected, and you rule with dignity, compassion, and gentle guidance. BUT with all that said, you're not putting up with any shenanigans from your furry child. As Benevolent Dictator, Top Dog, Big Dog, Alpha Dog, Mother Dog, Daddy Dog (whichever crown you prefer to wear), you're there to help your new pooch make good choices when it comes to her manners. When she can comprehend that what she's doing (a) pleases you and (b) gets her a treat, praise, or a reward for good behavior, she'll make every effort to comply. After all, when Big Dog is happy, everybody's happy.

Welcome to Basic Training—Class Is Now in Session

Photo Courtesy of Peter Hilton

You may have already decided that you'd prefer not to train your dog yourself, and instead enroll him in a dog obedience class. Perfect. Whatever works for you, your family members, and your dog. Or you may have decided to DIY—do it yourself. No matter which method you're choosing, the training basics should begin when your dog is comfortable in his new home. That doesn't mean as soon as he walks through the front door for the first time. Once he's had a chance to settle in a bit, sniffs everything that needs to be sniffed, and checks out his new digs, you can start by reinforcing his good behavior. Even the youngest dog will understand praise, especially if it's in the form of a treat. He goes into his crate on his own? Your lighthearted voice tells him,

CHAPTER 8   Where Are Your Manners?

"What a good boy!" or, "Here's a treat for going in your crate!" Positive reinforcement is essential to everything that he does well, from relieving himself outside, to finding his water bowl. No matter how small the deed, praise his good efforts.

Whether your Airedale is a puppy or an older dog whom you've adopted, your first step in the training process should be to teach him his name. Use it frequently, in a light, positive tone of voice when speaking to him. As soon as he acknowledges you, lavish him with praise or a treat. Repeat the process every chance you get. Familiarity with his name is not only important in the training process, but can also be a matter of safety, especially if you need to get his attention quickly.

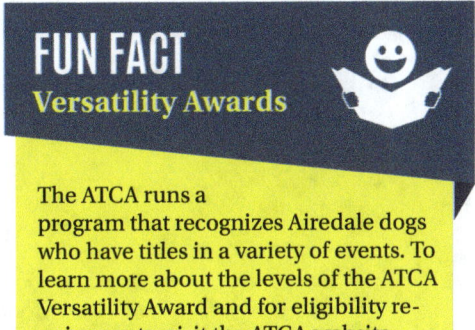

FUN FACT
Versatility Awards

The ATCA runs a program that recognizes Airedale dogs who have titles in a variety of events. To learn more about the levels of the ATCA Versatility Award and for eligibility requirements, visit the ATCA website.

Never associate his name with negatives. Ever. If he knocks over his water bowl, it's much better to address the situation with, "Oh, what happened?" in a disappointed tone of voice, than to angrily scream, "Max! Bad dog! Look what you did!" If your dog seems to be uninterested, or simply doesn't yet understand the concept, keep his leash attached. If he's not ready to respond to his name, give a little tug on the leash to bring him to you. Add distractions, bring him into another room, or take him outside for a change of scenery and keep trying. But don't try so much that your dog is becoming bored. Puppies especially have a very short attention span, so limit the number of repetitions, and try it again later.

Use the same process with older dogs, but here we would advise to use an even gentler tone of voice. If you've adopted your Airedale, you may not know what his history involved before he came to his new home. If his owners used his name for punishing a behavior, or association with any sort of abusive treatment, he may be fearful when he hears his name. Praise, treats, rewards for good behavior. A+ for good effort. And a soft, encouraging voice that says, "We love you and you're safe in our home."

A note here regarding all that praise and encouragement: Just as you keep your voice calm and relaxed when you're disappointed, giving a command, or correcting an unwanted behavior, praise should also be offered in a relaxed, quiet manner. There's no need to respond with a thunderous round of applause or a loud and excited voice. Stay on an even keel, and keep the atmosphere soothing and comfortable for your dog. Show him

Photo Courtesy of Mindy Turk

your approval, praise his behavior, but leave out the bells and whistles, and save the happy dance for later.

Since you'll be offering treats often, use very small training treats. If your dog loves vegetables, fruit, or cheese, and you'd prefer to use human foods such as these for training, be sure it's something that is healthy for your dog, and give very small pieces when rewarding his efforts. Occasionally, trainers may recommend that you substitute treats with a favorite toy or some playtime. However, you'll need to take a break from the training session while your dog plays with that toy. I like to wait until after the session to give a toy as a reward. Small treats provide more immediate gratification.

Along with a supply of training treats (those little bits that you'll be giving her often), keep some "high value" treats on hand as well. Those are the very special treats that you won't be offering her on a regular basis for training sessions, but the treats that she will come to learn mean, "You did something REALLY amazing." Or, "This required a lot more effort on your part and you've done a great job." She'll get the idea.

If you repeatedly use a specific word or phrase when your dog does something good, along with a treat, he will understand quickly that the

CHAPTER 8 Where Are Your Manners?

word or phrase means he's done something good. But you can also use the same process when he's done something that exhibits a negative behavior. Just saying "No" may not be as effective as using a disapproving tone of voice with a phrase such as, "That's not a good thing," or just a simple "Uh-oh, I'm not happy." It won't come across as quite so harsh, but he'll understand. If he's really committed a major felony, you can also give him a time-out, but make it brief. After a minute or so, he'll have no idea what he's done that's brought about your displeasure.

Photo Courtesy of Ruth Antoniuk

CHAPTER 9
The Commands

The Sit Command

The first command to teach your dog, and one of the easiest for him to learn, is "Sit." Get your treats ready, and work with your dog in a room where there are no distractions. Keep a short leash and flat collar on your dog when training him, as you'll be able to give him a gentle "attention tug" if need be. Plan to keep your training sessions short—5 to 10 minutes is ideal. The number of times you work with your dog will depend upon his attention span. Two or three times a day is preferable for consistency.

Photo Courtesy of Chelsea Alger

Show your dog the treat, hold it above his nose (within a few inches at most), and then move the treat up over his head. At the same time, say, "sit" in a quiet tone. If he doesn't sit, gently guide his back end down with your hand. When he sits, praise him by repeating, "Good sit." and immediately allow him to have the treat. It may take several weeks until your dog gets the idea of what you're asking him to do. Don't give up, don't yell or get frustrated. Continue with short sessions and lots of praise when he responds to what you're asking.

If your dog seems unusually inattentive, check to see if the actual area in which you're working is not causing him to become distracted. Some dogs work better on different surfaces, so be sure he's not bothered by an unfamiliar or stiff carpet, or a cold or rough floor. And by all means, see if he's enjoying the treats you're offering. Perhaps he's just not into those peanut butter–flavored training nuggets. Some dogs have a more sophisticated palate than others.

CHAPTER 9   The Commands

When you're sure he understands the sit concept, try using it before you open the door to go for a walk, when you're ready to take him out for some exercise or playtime, when he's not paying attention, or when he's distracted. (If he's going out for a bathroom break, however, it's more important to get him out quickly.) Remember to praise and/or reward! Later, you can also use specific hand commands to go along with a verbal "sit." (As a hand command for "sit," I cup my hand slightly and use a sweeping right to left half-circular motion.) For the time being, though, it's best not to overwhelm him. Keep his training sessions simple, short, and end them on a positive note. And keep it fun.

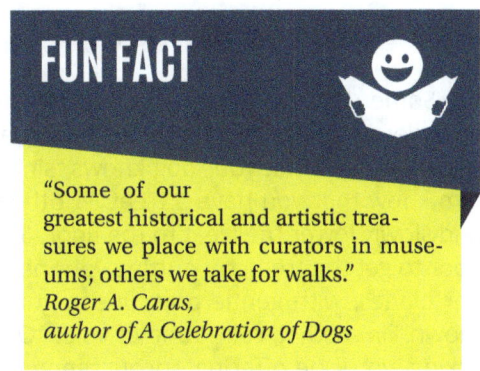

FUN FACT

"Some of our greatest historical and artistic treasures we place with curators in museums; others we take for walks."
Roger A. Caras,
author of A Celebration of Dogs

"OK" a.k.a. "Release"

It's good to have one word that your dog will understand when your command and his action have been completed. Start on this early, but in a more informal way.

Photo Courtesy of Luke Slater

Decide what word you feel comfortable using. A simple "OK" is my preferred release word. Just be consistent so he'll realize that this is his word to relax, and recognize that he's off command. Stay away from words that could confuse him. If you're releasing him from a command and say, "Good boy," he may not be able to figure out whether or not he's finished, and can now go play with his toys, or if you're praising him and he's still working. Your release word is just as important as your command word, so try and get it into the training routine as early as possible without too much confusion on the part of your dog.

The Down Command

Some dogs find the "down" more difficult than the sit command. It's considered a submissive stance for him, and can take a little extra time and patience. Now that your dog knows "sit," give him the sit command, and let him know that you have a treat. Put the treat a few inches from his nose, and slowly lower the treat to the floor. If he doesn't lower his belly onto the floor to get the treat, try putting your hands on his back between his shoulder blades, with gentle pressure to guide him down, all the while saying, "down," in a quiet, calm tone of voice. Of course, as he's doing what you're asking, you'll be offering encouragement and praise. If he's resisting, you can also use his flat collar and leash to prompt him into a down position. Again, use gentle guidance and a light touch. As soon as your dog's belly is on the floor, immediately give him his treat and lots of praise.

In conjunction with the verbal "down" command, when your dog is ready, add the hand command for "down." I use a flat hand motion, palm facing downward, while repeating the word "down." When he's done what you've asked, say "OK!" to release him, praise and offer a treat. Note: Once your dog is familiar with the down command, your goal should be to train him to go directly from standing to "down" and eventually eliminate the "sit" as the initial part of the down command. But as he's still in the early learning stages, it's physically easier for him to go from a sit to down.

The Stay Command

If your dog is Ms. Perpetual motion, she most likely will not take too kindly to the "stay" command. Initially, you'll need to adjust to her attention span and use many short training sessions until she becomes familiar with "stay." Although the "stay" command may be more difficult for your dog to master, look at it this way—this is the one command that could save your dog's life. My dog is a weekly client at our local doggy daycare facility, where she loves to play with her canine friends. Her tail is wagging and she's very excited to get there. BUT...her doggy daycare is in a strip mall on a very busy street. As her dog mom, I know that she's chomping at the bit to get inside to meet and greet all her buddies. I can't take a chance on having her jump out of the car as soon as the door is open, get distracted, and run into the street. So when that car door is unlocked, without hesitation on my part, she hears "STAY," and does not move from her seat until I have her leash attached to her collar and firmly in my hand, and release her with an enthusiastic "OK!" Even though she knows she's supposed to stay, I'm not assuming that she will.

If your dog is walking in a park with you, and she's off leash, and she spots a deer or a squirrel, she needs to hear "STAY," unless you want her bounding into the woods after said critter. As soon as your dog is ready, this word should absolutely be an important part of her command vocabulary.

Give your dog the "sit" command. (For the "stay" command, I use the hand command that you'd use to signal "stop"—a flat palm out and facing your dog.) As you begin working on this command, you can use a flat collar and leash if you find it easier. Walk backwards a few feet away from her, all the while repeating "stay." If she gets up to follow you, bring her back to where she was sitting, say, "sit," then "stay," once again with the hand command. Walk backwards and a few feet away from her again. After a few seconds, say, "OK" or whatever word you've chosen as a release word, and praise and/or give her a treat.

You can also have your dog on a "down" instead of a "sit" if it's less stressful for her, but you should eventually be working with a "down—stay" command. When she's proficient with this, you can simply move to "stay" from wherever or however she is positioned. Increase the length of time that she's in "stay" gradually. Later, if you're working with her as a means to keep her from leaving the car, an enclosed garage works well. If she rides in the rear seat, tell her "stay" before you get out of the car to come around to leash her and take her out. Learning "stay" requires patience, but the amount of practice time and effort involved will ultimately be worth it.

> **FUN FACT**
> **Barn Hunting**
>
> Barn Hunt is a relatively new sport for dog breeds who have a history of hunting vermin, such as the Airedale. Barn Hunt was created by Robin Nuttall and her Min Pin, Zipper. Prior to 2014, Min Pins were not allowed to compete in AKC Earthdog competitions, so Nuttall created this sport. The sport consists of a maze of hay bales with hidden rats and rat bedding within. Dogs are timed and compete in three height divisions. No rats are killed during the hunt. The Barn Hunt Association is an independent organization, but Barn Hunt titles may be listed on AKC pedigrees. For more information, visit www.barnhunt.com.

The Recall

This is another command that your dog MUST learn, and she must learn to do it whatever the circumstances. Again, it could be a life-saver. Having a dog who does not respond to your command of "come" is potentially putting her (and possibly YOUR) life in danger. She could also be at risk of wandering away and getting lost, and at best, is saying, "Hey, there's something I'm really interested in over here, and I'm ignoring you because you're just not as important." SO, let's address the priorities by realizing that the "come," or recall, command is never, ever negotiable. But we'll do it in the most rewarding, fun, enthusiastic way so your dog doesn't even hesitate for a second when he's being called. Your dog's mindset when working on the recall should be that when he hears "come!" there will be the best-ever, most wonderful reward or praise waiting for him when he gets to you.

If you sometimes tire or lose some interest in so much dog training, work with your dog when you can stay upbeat, energetic, and totally committed to your dog's training because the outcome will be a dog who's well-mannered, responsive, and who can't wait to be by your side. Break out those high value, special treats that he absolutely loves, and for which he will do anything. He needs to know that "come!" means a totally spectacular reward is waiting for him. Got it?

CHAPTER 9   The Commands

About those "special" treats: Some dog trainers have reported great success using cheese bits (especially string cheese cut into bite-sized pieces), small bits of cooked meat and chicken, and there are trainers who wholeheartedly endorse using Cheerios breakfast cereal. The pieces are small, the dogs love them, and they won't add too many extra calories to your dog's daily diet.

When you're ready to work on the recall with your Airedale, pick a time of day when he's relaxed, has no distractions (kids, toys, noise, etc.), and has already had his bathroom break. Bring him into a fairly roomy space where you can work with him uninterrupted. Feel free to put his flat collar and leash on. Have his special treats handy. Give him the commands to sit and stay, followed by a treat and praise when he complies. Now take a few steps backwards, and give him the command, "Come!" (The hand signal I use is to wave my palm toward my chest area.) If he doesn't respond, you can walk toward him, pick up his leash, and walk backwards to the spot where you originally stood, all the while saying "come" in a calm, happy voice. Treat time.

Next, have him sit and stay in that spot, walk away, and repeat. Do not praise him or offer a treat if he only gets halfway to you, but encourage him to come all the way. He needs to be within an arm's reach of where you want him. Practice, practice, but only as long as he's interested and responsive. If he's getting tired or bored, take a break and come back to it at a later time. But don't abandon the ship. Your Airedale is independent, and can be pretty darned stubborn when he wants to be. He's smart. But you're smarter. Plus, you've got the treats.

When you're confident that he understands the recall, it's time to take him outside. You can start working with him around distractions, and there's no better place than being outside. There's a plethora of smells, sounds, and everything that makes life interesting for an Airedale. Your job is to get him to focus on you, and what you're asking him to do. To assist him in this new endeavor, attach a long rope (20 feet or so) to his flat collar. Ask him to sit and stay, give him a treat. Now walk to the end of the rope, and say, "Come." If he's not responding or too busy checking out the surrounding scenery, you can gently reel him in toward you, all the while saying, "Come." When he's within arm's reach, praise and offer that special treat. Remember, it's not easy for him to multi-task: there's a bird flying overhead, there's a car horn beeping somewhere, his feet are making funny noises on the ground, and you're asking him to come to your side, all at the same time. When he does what you need for him to do, give him another treat and some extra praise.

A cautionary word here: Do not, under any circumstances, allow your dog off leash (unless he's in an enclosed area) until you are 100% sure that you can trust him with the recall! It may take months of work. A dog who responds to "come" 99% of the time is a dog who should still be on a leash when on walks, playing outside, or on outings. Sorry, but that one percent of the time is one percent too many. Don't take the risk.

The Heel Command

You've most likely watched a televised dog competition, and have admired the dogs who majestically trot by their handler's side, totally focused on staying in step. Why doesn't the average dog on the street do this? Well, my dog was not, is not, and never will be, a show dog. She goes for numerous walks every day, knows better than to pull on her leash (for the most part) and just for the record, she can do a decent "heel" when I ask her to. But I'm lazy, she's sweet, and we usually are too busy taking a leisurely stroll and chatting with other dog people.

Winter here in New England, however, can get messy, and with snow piles and limited sidewalk access, we occasionally do need to implement the "heel" command. Some folks find this command totally unnecessary, but I disagree. Your dog absolutely should know how to heel because (1) when you ask her to "heel" you're reinforcing your Alpha Dog status; you ask, she complies; (2) it contributes to her mental stimulation; she's exercising her brain and thinking about what she should be doing; (3) if you've practiced this command with your dog enough, chances are very good that she won't be tempted to pull ahead of you on walks; if you've got physical limitations or walkways are icy, you don't want her to be the cause of your emergency trip to the hospital, and (4) if you've got a pocket full of treats with which to reward her, she'll be a very happy dog.

Here's how to practice the "heel" command: As with her other training sessions, begin working in a quiet environment with no distractions. Have a flat collar and leash on the dog, and some training treats. Walk with your dog close by your side, with no slack in the leash. You will want her next to your leg. Repeat the command "Heel" as you walk, then stop quickly. Give her the sit command, and when she sits, give her a treat and praise. Tell her "OK" or whatever your release word is, and as she gets up, immediately say "heel" and repeat by walking with her at your side.

Keep it fun so that she's enjoying the process, and use plenty of treats and praise. It will most likely take some time for her to completely understand, but when you're convinced that she's "got it," start working with her outside. If you use just a few "heel" commands every time you go for a stroll, she'll always be ready to walk at your side. One additional note: All training should be done with a 6-foot leash. Please don't even THINK of using a retractable leash for any of the training commands.

You may be curious as to why some trainers and dog show handlers will insist that dogs "must" heel on the left side. It's all due to that famous catch-all word, tradition. It's been said that heeling dates back to olden days, when hunters would train their dogs to stay on their left side, for the simple reason that they carried their guns on their right side. At least that's one theory. Depending upon which side of the street I'm walking on, I will have my dog heel on the side away from traffic. If you're more comfortable with your Airedale walking on one side or the other, rest assured that the Heeling Police will probably not issue your dog a ticket for non-compliance.

The Drop It Command

Every dog should be taught to respond to "Drop it." Whether he's got a toy, a tasty potentially poisonous morsel that he's just dug up from your garden, or your expensive Manolo Blahnik high-heeled shoe between his chops, "drop it" should be an essential training command in your dog's vocabulary. In his mind, this command will reinforce your status as Top Dog, but it also may save his life (and possibly the life of your favorite shoe).

Give your dog a toy, or something that catches his interest, but not anything as enjoyable as his favorite training treat. As he's fully focused on the toy, say, "Drop it," offer him the treat instead, and when he does drop it, give him some enthusiastic praise and the special treat. This command will take some practice, but he'll soon understand. Never pull the toy out of his mouth. He should be letting go of it willingly. Because Big Dog said so.

Physical and Mental Exercise

Your Airedale Terrier is not only extraordinarily smart and extremely good looking. He's also quite an athlete. In the human sphere, he'd be a candidate for an Ivy League college, the distinguished recipient of a few prestigious scholarships, and a quarterback or pitcher who's being scouted for the majors. Or reasonable facsimile. In other words, your Airedale's got what it takes to be a great dog.

But it doesn't end with the sit, down, come, stay, heel, and drop it commands. You've got to provide both the physical AND mental exercise that he needs, because a bored Airedale can spell "T-r-o-u-b-l-e". That trouble could take various forms, none of which you're going to appreciate: digging, aggression, behavioral problems, barking, separation anxiety, to name but a few. Physically, Airedales are fairly high-energy dogs, but not categorically hyperactive. They just need a bit more mental and physical stimulation than some other breeds.

Although your dog may be a whiz at responding to your commands, you'll also need to provide him with "jobs." Yes, jobs. Your Airedale can easily learn the "names" of his favorite toys, so teach him to "get" his bunny or his binky. Once he understands the name for it, he'll be happy to fetch his beloved stuffed toy, and if you've provided him with a toy box, he can help put his belongings away when asked. Play a shell game with him by hiding treats under those big red plastic cups and telling him to "find it." Stash a few treats or toys around the house and play hide and seek. Dogs love bubbles, so head to the Dollar Store and purchase a few bottles. If your Airedale loves the water, as most do, a small plastic kiddie pool will provide hours of entertainment, weather permitting. (The key word here is "MOST." When taken to the beach or a lake, my Airedale, upon seeing the water, would immediately head in the opposite direction.)

CHAPTER 9   The Commands

Photo Courtesy of
Vanna Noisy Hawk

And there are always the old standbys that your dog will love—no self-respecting Airedale ever turned down a good game of fetch. Some dogs love to play Frisbee. You can teach your dog fun tricks. (Contrary to popular belief, you CAN teach an old dog new tricks.) Pet stores and the internet offer a wealth of interactive dog toys. Tennis balls will provide hours of amusement (especially the Kong brand with the squeakers), and when combined with a ball launcher, you've got instant playtime. (Caution: a fenced in area is a must.)

As athletic as Airedales are, however, if your new dog is a puppy, you'll need to start slowly. A puppy's bones and joints are still forming until the age of approximately 18 months, so while you don't need to be a doggy helicopter parent and fear that every movement will cause skeletal or muscular damage, you should also give him age-appropriate exercise and activity. Consulting with your veterinarian is your best course of action.

When your vet agrees that your dog is at the proper age and stage of his development, agility training may be perfect for your dog. Airedale Terriers love the physical as well as the mental challenges of this type of exercise. If you vary the routine, he'll never get bored and will love working alongside of you. A professional course or an agility training center is ideal, but as an alternative, you can improvise at home by placing objects for him to be taught to go in, under, around, and through. The possibilities are endless, but first and foremost, keep your dog's safety and physical condition in mind. Begin slowly, and don't overdo it. At the end of your session, you'd like a dog who's tired, but happy, and not one who is suffering from exhaustion.

CHAPTER 10
The Importance of Socializing

"It's always better and easier to start socializing as a puppy. Get them around lots of other dogs and animals while they are still young. As an adult, use supervision and commands while introducing them to a new animal. Give them time and be sure they are doing well together before you trust them alone together. Read their body language!"

Anne Ramseyer
Annes Airedales LLC

In human terms, most Airedales are extroverts. They're an outgoing, sociable, curious breed, and if they were people, they'd probably be the ones you'd want to invite to your parties. There's never a dull moment when there's an Airedale around. But similar to some people we know, they need to be taught the proper etiquette of how to behave in social situations. Just because you're having a good time, doesn't mean there aren't boundaries that need to be respected, and that also applies to your dog. If your Airedale barks at people, jumps on them, growls, counter-surfs, begs at the dinner table, or exhibits any number of annoying behaviors, you'll need to educate him on proper doggy etiquette.

Photo Courtesy of Carly Kanipe

CHAPTER 10   The Importance of Socializing

Introducing Your Airedale to People, Places, and Things That Go Bump in the Night

Dogs are most impressionable between 4 weeks old and 4 months old. If your Airedale enters your life as a young dog, this is the absolute best time to begin introducing him to the world. It's a scary place out there for a puppy. Acclimating your furry friend to the sights, sounds, and smells of everything new and previously unknown to him is one of the most significant jobs for which you, his dog parent, will be responsible. Make it fun for him.

FUN FACT
WWI Hero

A British Airedale named Jack was responsible for saving his battalion during WWI. The unit was stranded, cut off, and in need of reinforcements. Despite multiple injuries, Jack was able to reach headquarters and summon reinforcements for his batallion, saving their lives at the cost of his own.

Check with your veterinary practice first, and be sure that your puppy has had all vaccinations necessary for him to be exposed to other dogs and new experiences. As soon as they give you the "go ahead," it's time to teach your dog that there's no need to be afraid of the wind, the sounds of trucks driving by, the kids riding their bicycles, meeting new dogs, and people walking by on the street.

Keep your attitude upbeat, positive, and encouraging. Go for walks, expose your dog to new adventures, but do it slowly. If you usually walk the same neighborhood with him, try a different route. If he's never been to a park, go for a brief outing there. Leashed, of course. Have a pocketful of treats. Be aware of his reactions to everything new and start reinforcing his positive response to different experiences. Give him the confidence to explore. Don't force him, don't overwhelm him, don't coddle him if he appears fearful, but offer encouragement and treats, and monitor your own reaction.

What many dog owners don't realize is that your dog is an expert at interpreting what's going on at the other end of his leash. That would be YOU. Example: If you encounter a new dog, you may automatically tense up and pull back (even slightly) on the leash. Your dog immediately thinks, DANGER! It doesn't take very much for your Airedale, no matter how young or old, to understand the signals that you're sending him. You may not realize it, but he certainly does. Watch his reaction, but be aware of your own as well.

Photo Courtesy of Michelle Dykstra

CHAPTER 10 The Importance of Socializing

Puppy Socialization Classes

Puppy socialization classes, sometimes called puppy kindergarten classes, are widely available, and can be one of the best ways to introduce your new Airedale to other puppies. Look for recommendations from other dog owners, or confer with your veterinarian on referrals to local facilities. Some puppy groups will invite you to attend without your dog first, just to become familiar with how it all works.

Puppy groups are run by trainers experienced in working with the many facets of young dog socialization as well as introducing your dog to basic commands. Your Airedale will get to meet other dogs, play, exercise, burn off a little of that puppy energy, and even learn some pretty interesting and fun new things. She will likely have an enjoyable session, and if you have any questions about your dog's behavior, the trainer/facilitator should be able to address your concerns. If special behavioral issues do exist, your trainer or puppy kindergarten facilitator might recommend that more individualized sessions could be beneficial. It's best to begin working on issues sooner rather than later. If there are no concerns, then your dog will have a great time, you may learn some new training techniques, and you both might even make some new friends. At the very least, your puppy will need a nice, long nap when she gets home.

Socializing Your Older Airedale Terrier with Other Dogs

Older dogs can sometimes present more challenges when it comes to socialization. If they've been in neglectful or abusive situations, or have just never been exposed to the concept of getting along with other dogs, you'll need to take it slowly. Taking your Airedale for long walks is a good way to acclimate her to social situations, but in a controlled way. With your dog on leash, you can keep the dynamics of dog-meets-dog from escalating into potentially aggressive contact if need be, and she'll still be experiencing new sights, sounds, and other dogs. She'll enjoy expending some energy, and it will also be a good opportunity to work on some basic commands. If you don't know your dog's personality well just yet, it's never a good idea to think, "Well, I'll just bring her to a dog park and she can make some new friends." That could be a recipe for disaster. Not only do you not know how your dog will react, but likewise, you don't know how other dogs will respond. They could be the aggressors, your dog could be injured, and if owners try to break up a dog fight, there could be human injuries as well. Please don't take a chance.

Another place where it's fairly easy to begin to socialize your dog is a pet supply store. Many stores encourage dog owners to bring their furry kids in when they shop, and as a new dog owner, you'll be a frequent visitor. Your Airedale will probably be delighted to pick out her own treats, as the sights and smells in a pet shop can obviously be quite tempting. So we'd encourage you to give it a try and keep the experience a positive one for her. Country fairs, farmer's markets, concerts in the park, and neighborhood gatherings are all places where dogs on leashes are usually welcome, so take advantage of possible doggy socialization opportunities as often as you can.

If you're walking her on leash and meet another dog who's also on leash, you should possess an upbeat, positive attitude, and convey an air of confidence to your dog, so she's comfortable with the whole getting-acquainted and socialization process. A pocketful of treats is great reinforcement for a successful neighborhood outing and a positive response to meeting other dogs.

Get to know your Airedale's physical cues. While you always want to maintain a calm demeanor, become familiar with what your dog is telling you with her body language. Despite what most people have been taught to believe, a wagging tail is not always the sign of a happy dog. It "usually" is, but it could also mean that she's nervous. Obvious signs of an anxious dog: her tail is tucked between her legs, the hair on her neck and back is standing up, she bares her teeth, growls, is panting, she has her ears pulled back, or is trembling. If she exhibits any of these behaviors, gently and calmly remove her from the situation. She's nervous, fearful, or just not sure of what's happening.

Be mindful that some dogs have issues with certain types of other dogs. She might be fine with dogs her own size or smaller, but terrified of bigger dogs. Some dogs are more aggressive toward dogs of the same or opposite sex, or unneutered males. Some older dogs or dogs with health issues may have little tolerance for young puppies. Be sensitive to where your dog fits into the mix, and understand that this could be a situation where consulting with a professional dog trainer would be a good option for both you and your dog. By all appearances, your older dog may not have any obvious "quirks," but it's possible that just one minor incident would set her off if it's a reminder of an unpleasant experience from her past.

CHAPTER 10   The Importance of Socializing

Photo Courtesy of Michael Rufe

Socializing Your Dog with People

Every dog has his own unique personality, along with his own unique relationship with his owner and human family. Your dog may be shy and timid, and take a few steps backwards when it comes to meeting strangers. He could become the canine version of a Velcro strap and attach himself to your leg. On the other hand, he may be the first one to charge ahead to say hello. The means of socializing your dog with people are basically the same rules that apply to introducing him to other dogs: exposure, exposure, exposure. The more people he gets to meet, the more he'll realize that it's not so scary. Let him go at his own pace, and don't force him to like everyone. You just don't want him to be aggressive, and that especially applies to being around children. Unless taught differently, kids tend to think that every dog is friendly. If you have any concerns about how your dog will react, stay one step ahead when a child approaches your dog, and quietly ask them not to pat him.

Personally, I don't care if my dog doesn't like everyone. I don't like everyone, either. But I'm not about to growl at strangers or threaten them in any way. I know enough to be pleasant, at the very least, and not provoke a confrontation. This should apply to your dog as well. He doesn't need to greet everyone with hand licks and tail wags, but proper etiquette dictates that he should at least not instigate a brawl. At a minimum, it's essential for him to be polite. If your Airedale shows signs of aggression or anxiety when approached, please consider contacting a professional trainer.

Just as some dogs are more timid around certain types of dogs, there are those dogs who act differently around certain types of people. While it can be seen as odd behavior, it's something to be aware of from the dog parent's perspective. I've known dogs who were afraid of tall men, short women, people of various ethnic backgrounds, loud children, etc. There are dogs who cower at elderly or disabled people walking with canes or crutches, babies in carriages, and people wearing any number of articles of apparel—hats, gloves, puffy jackets, scarves, backpacks. One dog I know is terrified of anyone he sees carrying a briefcase or a purse. Why? Who knows? Just because. Perhaps something traumatic in his history, or at some point, he may have been frightened by someone carrying a briefcase or purse. But if you're ready to put some time and effort into alleviating his "phobia" (for lack of a better word), it will help to make him a little more comfortable and not quite so fearful. Plus, it's good manners.

CHAPTER 10   The Importance of Socializing

Socialize your dog around as many different people as possible. Take him with you as much as you can. Let him see that people are not out to get him. The more humans he comes in contact with, the more likely he will be willing to let go of some of his fears. Keeping him away from people will only reinforce his anxiety. So be gentle, consistent, work with him at a slow and steady pace (have a pocket of treats!), and be committed to showing him that the world is not such a bad place.

Photo Courtesy of Colleen Standley

Benefits of Doggy Day Care to Socialize Your Dog

Way back in the good old days, if you wanted your dog to get some exercise, have a bathroom break, or play with a doggy friend, you'd simply open the front door, let him out to wander the streets aimlessly for hours on end, and figure that he'd come back home when he was hungry. Those were also the days when many dogs actually didn't find their way back home, your odds of stepping in dog droppings on the sidewalk were all too high, and when and if your dog did return, he'd be sporting an injured paw or a gashed ear. If you even thought of sending your dog to doggy day care (which didn't exist in the "good old days"), you'd probably be sent for 30 days' observation at your local psychiatric facility. Come to think of it, why did we ever consider them "the good old days" anyway? They really weren't all that good, at least not from our dog's point of view. So now we have (drum roll, please) doggy day care, to which we wholeheartedly say, hallelujah.

What's so great about doggy day care? Pretty much everything, but only if (1) your dog is a good candidate, (2) you're happy with the facility, and (3) your dog is happy there. If you've chosen wisely, your canine companion will get plenty of exercise, interact with other dogs and humans, and be properly supervised. He'll have a chance to be independent (as in, without his dog parent) and overall, have a blast. In terms of socialization, doggy day care will provide your dog with hours of social skills. The benefits for your dog are immeasurable. The benefits for you, his owner, are many. You won't have to check your watch frequently because it's time for him to relieve himself. Or because he's been alone for too long. You won't have to worry that he's bored and may be tearing up your leather recliner. You'll have some freedom, and can be confident that little Ms. Airedale is having fun.

Most puppies seem to thrive at doggy day care facilities and they usually come home ready for a nice, long snooze at the end of their puppy day. But there may be some dogs who just don't do as well. If your puppy is very timid, it's not a good idea to throw him into a mix of curious, rambunctious dogs, all wanting to check out the "new kid." It can certainly be overwhelming for the doggy day care neophyte. If you've adopted an older dog, you'll need to know ahead of time how he'll respond to meeting the day care pack. He's here to have fun, but if it's causing stress, bringing out aggression, or making him nervous, then hiring a dog walker might be a better option. If your dog is very high-energy and gets "wound up" easily, a large doggy daycare facility may not be a good choice. For a dog who can

CHAPTER 10 The Importance of Socializing

become overstimulated by constant activity, a smaller day care center or private home day care might be best. One that provides shorter sessions is another consideration.

Some dogs are just happier lounging at home, and would actually PREFER not to be hanging out with 20 or 30 fellow canines. There are introverts and extroverts in the dog world. While most Airedales I've known, loved, and worked with tend to be outgoing and sociable, there are others who are happiest when their days are spent in quiet repose. Are you the type of person who would rather make yourself a cup of tea and read a book after dinner, or would you rather go dancing and stay out until the wee hours? Consider whether your Airedale is a dancer or a reader. Or somewhere in between.

Photo Courtesy of Betsy Burroughs

How to Choose a Doggy Day Care Facility

Get referrals. Speak with your veterinarian, other dog parents who bring their dogs to day care, and visit the facilities, first without your dog. Is it clean? Is the staff knowledgeable and friendly? First impressions are important. How many dogs are there on a typical day? Is it well supervised, and what is the staff-to-dog ratio? Are smaller dogs and bigger dogs kept separately? (The answer to that question should be a resounding "YES." You don't want your puppy in with a 150-pound Mastiff, no matter how friendly the big fellow might be. Injuries can happen, however unintentional.) Are the employees well trained?

Many doggy day care centers have fenced, outdoor facilities, so that in good weather, the dogs can be out in the fresh air. (My rescue dog loves to be in the water, and will spend hours in the summer just lounging in the kiddie pools that the staff provides.) Are the play rooms large enough to handle the number of dogs? Are there spaces where dogs can go to for some quiet time, when they need to be away from the hustle and bustle of daily play? What about hours of operation? Is there a half-day option? Some dogs just don't do well in an all-day situation. A long, tiring day (no matter how much fun) can cause your dog some stress if he's not used to that much activity.

Does the doggy day care facility have overnight and/or extended boarding, and is there someone who stays with the boarders all night? Many centers now offer a video stream, so that you can check from your home computer or mobile devices to see what your dog is up to. It's great to pop in for a virtual visit once in a while, but we'd caution you that too much viewing time is not a good idea. Dogs have their own language, and what you might interpret as aggressiveness may simply be that this is how your Airedale and his friends are playing. If the technology is available, that's nice, but don't hover.

What about pricing? Most facilities in our area charge competitive rates, with the average about $25–$30 for a whole day (8 hours), and $15–$20 for half day of 4 hours. If you'd like some socialization and playtime for your dog, but don't want to leave him for extended periods, some facilities offer a "drop-in" alternative, where you're able to bring your dog for just an hour or so, at a minimal rate, usually $5–$10. Some ask that owners remain with their dogs, while others will offer supervision. If an hour of playtime is enough for your dog, this could be a good option.

If you think that the larger doggy day care facility would not be beneficial for your Airedale, there are some doggy day care providers, usually in private homes, where 4 or 5 dogs can spend playtime together. For those dogs who enjoy some canine companionship, but on a quieter and more limited basis, this may be a good fit. Again, check references, cleanliness, in-

CHAPTER 10 The Importance of Socializing

surance, rules and regulations, and, if dogs are allowed outdoors, are they in a safe, well-contained area?

Professional dog walkers are available in most neighborhoods, and many provide services for both private and group walks. Some will take their doggy clients for hikes in the woods, to the beach, or on field trips. Again, check references, their level of experience, and what they offer.

If you've decided that a doggy day care center would benefit your dog, you'll be invited to bring her in for an initial evaluation. Staff members will ask you to fill out an application with pertinent information regarding your dog's personality and history. Before any evaluation takes place, you will need to provide a copy of your dog's vaccination and medical history. The staff will put your dog through some paces to see how she responds. Is she shy? Nervous? Or is she ready to get in there and make some new friends?

You will usually be asked to leave your dog for a period of time, which could vary from an hour to a half day. (Many facilities will offer the evaluation and first visit at no charge.) The staff will bring in one of their more laid-back, regular client dogs, or a staff member's dog, for a meet and greet, to see how your dog responds. They will evaluate for sociability, aggressiveness, submissiveness, and overall temperament. If it's a "go," your dog will be welcome to come play, and enjoy all that doggy day care has to offer.

But...if it's a "no," don't take it personally. A responsible doggy day care facility will not let any dog attend if there's even the slightest chance that he may be putting himself or other dogs in danger of being injured. A well-run, conscientious, professional center would rather turn a prospective client away than put any of their dogs at risk.

If doggy day care is the right fit for your dog, here's one more bit of advice: It's a good idea to be sure your Airedale receives a regular flea and tick preventative treatment, and is up to date on kennel cough and flu shots. No matter how clean or careful a doggy day care provider is, diseases can still be spread from one dog to another. Some, but not all, doggy day care facilities require these preventative measures, while for others it's optional.

Not every doggy day care facility will be a good match for every dog. My own rescue pup, who is one of the sweetest, most laid-back dogs I've ever owned, was turned down at one of our local doggy day care centers after her initial evaluation. The reason? She wasn't aggressive, her behavior was fine, but she "really didn't contribute much to the pack." Well then. We tried another day care center, where she was evaluated, welcomed with open paws, and she's been a once or twice a week "regular" there for 6 years. She loves going, and they love having her. She fits in nicely, she comes home tired after a day of fun, and she's a happy girl.

CHAPTER 11
Surviving the Teen Years

Our focus thus far has been on the new puppy and the more mature Airedale. But we certainly can't leave out what happens in between—otherwise known as "The Teenager." And just like human teenagers, living with an adolescent dog can be frustrating, challenging, and chock-full of ups and downs. But make no mistake—there's lots of fun to be had, as well!

Between the ages of 6 months and 2 years old, your Airedale is undergoing many changes. He's not quite a puppy, but neither is he a mature adult dog. He's now comfortable in his surroundings, and he knows where he fits in to the family dynamics.

Physically, his little body is going through changes. He's getting his adult coat and may be shedding his baby fur. He may still be losing some baby teeth, but his adult teeth are almost all in, and his gums could be sore. He might be chewing on everything that he shouldn't. (Remember that trick with the wet, frozen sock or washcloth? This is a great time to use it to re-

CHAPTER 11 Surviving the Teen Years

lieve those sore gums.) Females will begin to go into heat, males will begin lifting their legs to mark their territory, and aggressive tendencies may begin to appear. It's all due to hormones.

Follow your veterinarian's recommendations for the best time to spay or neuter, usually done before your dog is 6 months old. It's generally believed that dogs who are spayed or neutered have much less chance of developing cancers, urinary tract infections, and thought to have a longer life expectancy than unsterilized dogs. Territorial marking, aggression, roaming and behavioral issues can also be greatly diminished. Unless you're planning to breed your Airedale, spaying or neutering should certainly be considered, but if you're still undecided, we urge you to consult with your veterinarian.

Your teenage dog is now at the stage where he's starting to question and have second thoughts about everything you've ever taught him: "So how come YOU'RE big dog?" "You're not the boss of me!" "There's a dog over there, and I need to go check her out." "Just because you're asking me to sit, I don't have to." "Oh, treats. No big deal. I'd rather go sniff that tree." "Think I'll go terrorize the cat." If your Airedale has been on his best behavior so far, responding positively to his commands, and generally being your sweet fur ball, get ready for some changes. They may be slight, and almost unnoticeable at first, and then, one day, POOF! Meet Dr. Jekyll and Mr. Hyde.

Photo Courtesy of Carly Kanipe

The good news is that this phase won't last too long, and you'll have your cuddly little cherub back. The bad news is that you'll have to do some work.

As for my own experience with my teenage "Airedale Terror," the first clue we had that she was reaching adolescence occurred one night, as we were quietly relaxing on the couch, watching TV, as we usually did after dinner. We suddenly observed our formerly laid-back, couch potato of a dog get up from her doggy bed, yawn, stretch, and then proceed to race in circles around the house. She completed about 15 laps, retired to her bed, and promptly fell asleep. That incident, which became a nightly routine, was then followed by months of Murphy totally forgetting (or ignoring) everything she'd previously learned, acquiring all sorts of not so charming new habits and hobbies (digging, jumping on people, chewing on furniture), and becoming an overall royal pain in the butt. Murphy's formerly few misdemeanors were quickly becoming frequent felonies, and so it was off to the dog trainer. (Point of information: That sporadic racing around the house is technically known as "FRAPS"—Frenetic Random Activity Periods. Also called "zoomies." It's very common for puppies and teenaged dogs to engage in this somewhat bizarre behavior, and just their weird way of burning off extra energy. Watching a dog with the zoomies is actually somewhat entertaining. Their eyes may glaze over, they'll get a weird look on their face, and they could appear as if they're possessed by some otherworldly spirit. In any case, it's not harmful, and they'll outgrow it as they get a little older.)

Your Airedale's teenage phase involves a lot of testing on his part. This is the time you'll want (and need!) to start reinforcing basic commands. He may be growing weary of the "good boy, here's a treat" routine, so break out those high value treats as extra incentive. A chicken or cheese tidbit will entice when the sweet potato–flavored biscuits might have lost their appeal.

But don't stop there. It's time to boost the training mode up to high. Your dog hasn't forgotten his training, but he's now realizing that there's a whole lot of fun and exciting things out there in the world, and he's ready to explore. That's not a bad thing at all, but you'll still need to keep reminding him of who's in charge. Add some commands to his daily routine: Before he dives into his dinner, have him sit. If he loves going for car rides, give him a down command before you open the vehicle door. If he's out for a walk, spend some time on the heel command, then let him have fun sniffing those hydrants.

Photo Courtesy of Erin Probst

A teenage Airedale is experiencing a plethora of changes—both physically and psychologically. His energy level is at its peak. He's not sleeping

CHAPTER 11 Surviving the Teen Years

Photo Courtesy of Barbara Whitefield

nearly as much as he did as a puppy. He's meeting new friends, and even though he puts on a brave face, he's still a bit anxious about all these new experiences. His body is continuing to develop. The Airedale breed is known to have very rapid growth spurts, and as such, they often develop "panosteitis," commonly known as growing pains, particularly in their teenage phase. Your dog may be perfectly fine one minute, and for no apparent reason, begins limping, or exhibiting some pain in his joints. He could become lethargic, run a fever, or have a sudden change in appetite. If your Airedale exhibits any of these symptoms, a visit to your veterinarian is in order. Growing pains usually resolve within a short period of time, but it's always best to have a medical consult. Combined with everything else that your dog is going through as he becomes a teenager, is it any wonder he's a little befuddled these days?

You're still very much the center of his world. But for the teenage Airedale, that world has suddenly become a lot different. Be gentle with him. Don't go overboard with punishment or try to be overbearing in your role as Alpha Dog. He's at a very impressionable age. He may, at times, be downright obnoxious. With continued guidance and a lot of love and patience, you'll both get through the difficult days.

CHAPTER 12

Do You Need a Professional Dog Trainer?

Too many people are under the (mistaken) impression that a professional dog trainer is only necessary for dogs with aggression issues. Nothing could be further from the truth. Yes, if your dog is showing any signs of aggression, whether it's toward people or other animals, you should most definitely get thee to a trainer, ASAP. But there are many other reasons to work with a trainer: (1) You've never had a dog, and are not sure if what you're doing is correct. You just need a little guidance. (2) You'd like

CHAPTER 12 Do You Need a Professional Dog Trainer?

to socialize your new puppy, but would like some supervised playtime. (3) You've worked on basic commands, but would like to take it a little further. (4) Your dog isn't paying attention to you. (5) Your family members are not consistent with training the dog. Everyone's doing something different. (5) Your dog is tearing up the house, eating shoes, unruly. (6) His housetraining is not going well. (7) He won't let anyone near him when he's eating. (8) He's barking too much. (9) He howls when you leave the house. (10) He's pushy with other dogs. (11) Your dog urinates whenever someone comes into the house. (12) He jumps on everyone. (13) He's afraid of everything. (14) He pulls on the leash when you try to walk him. (15) You've had dogs before, but just need a refresher course on training. (16) You've adopted a dog, and he's got some quirky behaviors. (17) Your dog won't stop nipping at the kids. (18) Your Airedale has decided that his one and only job is to protect you from anything that he assumes could possibly cause you harm—the letter carrier, the pizza delivery guy, your mother-in-law. And that's just for starters. We can think of a zillion other reasons to contact a dog trainer, but you get the idea.

I love watching those DIY home remodeling shows on TV. They're chockfull of great ideas and how-to projects: "I think we need some hot pink paint to make the dining room walls pop." "We're putting in some new shrubs to perk up the landscaping." "Shiplap! We need shiplap!" Although many people are handy, and can manage do-it-yourself home improvement projects on their own, the flip side is that, without calling in a professional, it can be costly at best, an all-out catastrophe at worst. You just tore down a wall in your kitchen. Did you check to see if it was a bearing wall first? Oh-oh. Better call a professional, quickly! Where are we going with this? We're comparing do-it-yourself dog training with working with a professional.

If you're knowledgeable about the ins and outs of training a dog, if your Airedale happens to be a star student, and you're happy with her obedience, socialization skills, and dog/human bonding, then congratulations! You're one of the few who definitely CAN do it yourself. But most pet parents are all too eager to look the other way when there's a behavioral issue. And then that minor issue takes on a life of its own—it just gets bigger and bigger, and at some point, it's no longer a minor glitch in their dog's behavior, but a major problem.

Sadly, too many dogs are turned into shelters when dog parents become overwhelmed and just can't deal with their pet's bad manners, or worse, serious behavioral concerns. Don't think of working with a professional dog trainer as a last resort. Think of it as a means of avoiding what could ultimately become a last resort situation.

Finding the Right Professional Dog Trainer

What kind of dog trainer do you need, and how do you find the best one? Just like the question of where do you find a veterinarian or doggy day care facility, the answer is, "begin by asking for referrals." Ask friends, your veterinarian, other dog owners, and then do some internet research. Call local animal shelters to see if they can make recommendations. Decide what your goals are. Do you have concerns about your dog's behavior? Is your dog in need of training for basic commands? Are you just starting out with a new puppy? You'll want to find a trainer who can help address your dog's individual needs.

Once you've narrowed down the search for a trainer, have a list of questions ready. That list should include, but not be limited to: What are your training methods? How long have you been a dog trainer and do you have any certifications? Where does the training take place? Do you offer group and/or individual classes? Do you encourage the whole family, including young children, to attend classes? What are your specialties? Can you come to my home to train? Do you provide training outdoors? What are your prices? Can you provide references? Do we need to purchase a specific number of classes? Do you offer boarding and training? What equipment will we need to purchase? Is there an initial evaluation? Is there a class size limit?

For those who have a specific behavioral concern, ask what experience they've had in working with dogs with this particular issue. If you have a puppy, ask what age they prefer the dog to be to start lessons. What experience does the dog trainer have working with Airedale Terriers? You may have more questions of your own. Don't be afraid to ask BEFORE you commit to working with any trainer. A good trainer will always be happy to answer any questions, explain their methods and philosophy, and will want you to feel comfortable and understand the process.

The most important aspect of any dog training program is the dog owner. That's YOU. You can send your dog off to a training camp or program where a trainer will work with your dog to teach it commands and good manners, and work on any issues or individual behavioral problems. But you, as your dog's parent, must also understand and learn what you'll need to do to ensure that your dog continues to be the best that he can be. You cannot assume that just because your Airedale has had 3 or 10 or 20 sessions with a dog trainer, she'll automatically know how to behave. She won't. Your professional dog trainer will be just as interested in teaching you all you need to know to work with your dog. I believe that fifty percent of the work that a professional dog trainer does is with your dog. The other fifty percent should be in working with you, the owner.

CHAPTER 12   Do You Need a Professional Dog Trainer?

Types of Dog Training

Puppy Training Classes

Puppy training classes are fun! Your dog will have a great time, and there will very likely be many other puppy parents in attendance, all ooh'ing and aah'ing at the adorable little fur balls. Puppy parents will be mentally comparing which dog is cutest, craziest, most relaxed. Which is most likely to succeed in driving their owners bananas? Who's got the most potential for number of time-outs? Who'll be the first to fall asleep in the car?

Photo Courtesy of Ruth Antoniuk

Although you might not think that there's much more going on here than ear pulling, nipping, butt sniffing, and rolling around on the floor, you'll be surprised at how much you AND your dog will learn during these puppy classes. Many pet supply stores and doggy day care centers, as well as professional training facilities, provide these classes, and they are usually well-attended and offered at very reasonable fees. Besides enjoying a professionally supervised environment for you dog to socialize with other dogs her own age, you and your Airedale will be able to work with a trainer experienced with all aspects of puppy behavior, who can answer all questions related to both their physical, behavioral, nutritional, and developmental characteristics and requirements.

Classes will usually address general concerns pertinent to young puppies such as play-biting and nipping, excessive chewing, jumping, housetraining, and basic obedience. Commands such as sit, down, come, drop it, and walking on a leash will be taught. Most puppy classes are generally offered for dogs 8 to 16 weeks of age, number of sessions will vary—most often 4 to 6 classes, and you'll be required to provide proof of initial vaccinations in order to register your dog.

This is the age when your puppy is learning so much, and it's the best time to continually reinforce all her new knowledge. Work with your dog on a continuing basis, keep your at-home training sessions short but fre-

Photo Courtesy of Carly Kanipe

CHAPTER 12   *Do You Need a Professional Dog Trainer?*

quent, give her plenty of positive feedback, and above all, make it fun for both of you. Training your pup can be a wonderful bonding experience for you and your dog.

Beyond Puppy Training Class

You're determined to have a well-trained, well-mannered, respectful dog. Good for you! You've been working diligently with your dog, reinforcing basic commands, he seems to be doing well (for the most part), listening and learning, and you're both ready to take it to the next level. So what are your options? More training!

Remember that chapter on "Surviving Your Dog's Teen Years"? Some advanced training is a great way to continue with all you've been working on, and keep that dog/human bond growing. At 5 or 6 months old, this is the time in your dog's development when he's become pretty confident with himself, and with his environment. You've been working with him on his commands, he's relatively decent at a quick response, and... what's this? He's starting to hesitate ever so slightly when you call him because he's watching the leaves blow outside. Maybe he has to get in a few extra barks when you ask him to stop. (Oh, yes, lately he's decided he needs to have the last word, doesn't he?) Up until now, he's been great with his overall obedience. So great, in fact, that you've been slacking off a little bit. "Oh, he's such a good boy. I won't bother to correct him. It's just a teensy mistake."

This is a great opportunity to stay on top of things. Practice, practice, and practice some more. A professional dog trainer will be able to easily assess where your dog is in her training, what she (and you) need to work on, and where to go from there. You can take your Airedale's obedience training as far you'd like, including reinforcing what she already knows, eliminating a behavioral issue, teaching her new tricks and commands, or working toward having her earn her Canine Good Citizenship certification or perhaps become a therapy dog. Her training should remain a life-long learning experience. She'll be well-mannered, respectful, and a loving, joyful companion. What more could anyone ask for?

Photo Courtesy of Sarah M Bradbury

CHAPTER 13

Dealing with Unwanted Behavior – Your Dog's Bad Habits

"The #1 thing I hear from buyers (other than loving their puppy) is the biting. Airedale puppies are little terrors at time. They love to play and love to wrestle and use those little needle teeth on you. Some people that have never had an Airedale contact me concerned they have a really aggressive puppy. This is normal Airedale puppy behavior and time is the ultimate solution to this. The biting will lessen and go away with time"

Anne Ramseyer
Annes Airedales LLC

CHAPTER 13   Dealing with Unwanted Behavior - Your Dog's Bad Habits

It's easy to overlook or even completely ignore an Airedale's bad habits. Sometimes those "infractions" are so minuscule and innocent that we'll brush them aside: That cute little fluff ball is only being protective when he barks. Sure he's digging up the vegetable garden, but it's not a problem—the tomatoes weren't doing so well anyway. Oh, yes, he cries and howls when we leave him home alone, but he's just a baby. We make lots of excuses for our dog's irksome behavior, and then wonder how things plummeted downhill so quickly.

Bad habits happen to good dogs, and the longer we allow unwanted behaviors to continue, the more difficult they can be to stop. Let's take a look at some concerns of dog parents, and work on correcting and alleviating a few common dog misbehaviors.

Chewing

Although destructive chewing is not limited to dogs of a particular age, it's much more common with young puppies. They're teething, their gums hurt, it feels good to chew. Nothing is off limits, especially items that smell like their dog parent. Shoes, socks, underwear—all right up there on your Airedale's hit parade of favorite items to chew. What could be more embarrassing when guests are visiting, than seeing your puppy zipping through the living room, proudly carrying a pair of Dad's boxer shorts?

If you've been successfully working on the "drop it" command, your dog's random chewing issue is a good opportunity to start reinforcing. It's best to not use a treat for this one, however, because it could backfire. Your smart-as-a-whip Airedale could begin to reason that, "If I start chewing on something I'm not really supposed to have, they'll give me a treat instead." So here, we'll need to make the case for "Just drop it because I said so." Praise him when he gives up those boxer shorts, but let's not make too much of a big deal about it. He wasn't supposed to have them in the first place. Have plenty of toys on hand to substitute. Keep those toys in rotation. When you see your dog has become bored with some of his formerly favorite toys, put them away and bring them back out at a later date. He'll either be happy because he's forgotten about them and will think they're brand new, or he'll be happy because he's missed them. "My favorite stuffed bunny! Where have you been?"

Just as a toddler will get into things she shouldn't, your Airedale puppy will behave in a similar fashion. Best to remove all temptation, for his safety and your sanity. Spray furniture that your dog seems interested in with some Bitter Apple. Stuff some rubber chew toys with small treats for him to gnaw on. Spend extra time with your dog, and be sure that he's getting enough exercise, both mentally and physically, If he's bored, he'll be more likely to resort to chewing unacceptable objects. If he's stressed or lonely, he'll be more comforted with objects that belong to his human. He has no idea what's acceptable or unacceptable when it comes to chewing, so make a conscious effort to remove anything he shouldn't have, and substitute some chew-worthy, fun items that he'll enjoy sinking his teeth into. If you can't trust him alone, put him in his crate when you leave the house, along with plenty of acceptable items on which he can chew.

While this is usually a phase that most puppies will eventually outgrow, an older dog with a chewing habit can be more challenging. If you've recently adopted a teenager or a more mature dog, he may be experiencing some anxiety, nervousness, or stress. Have him checked by your veterinarian to be sure that there is no physical cause such as sore gums, a bad tooth, or a painful jaw. Any changes in the household routine, the addition of new pets or a new baby, a move, can all cause frustration and stress in your dog. Don't rule out boredom. I've had several dogs who were quite sensitive to changes in weather, and would exhibit anxiety with approaching thunderstorms or strong winds. Chewing provides comfort to a dog with any kind of anxiety.

The rules to reduce chewing problems in older dogs are the same as those which apply to puppies: remove all items which your Airedale may find tempting, give him plenty of acceptable chew toys, keep him in a crate if you're hesitant to leave him alone in the house, and be sure he gets plenty of exercise and mental stimulation. Do some detective work and try to figure out what's causing your dog's anxiety. Be sure that the chew toys you're providing are ones that he actually enjoys. If not, try adding some different textures and flavors to his selection. A little extra attention, more exercise, and some snuggles will always be a welcome addition to his daily routine.

Separation Anxiety

One of the most heartbreaking sounds that a dog parent may experience as they leave the house is their dog crying. Or whining. Or barking. It's commonly known as separation anxiety, and it's an issue that many of us have had to witness over our years of dog ownership. Research has shown that there are actually several different types of separation anxiety, and many different symptoms.

CHAPTER 13   Dealing with Unwanted Behavior - Your Dog's Bad Habits

One type is a separation anxiety that dogs actually learn, and an excellent example of this is one that puppies seem to be quite adept at achieving. You'll put your dog in her crate, make a fuss about going out, reassure her that you'll be right back, blow kisses and say, "be a good girl," and promise a treat when you return. She's got your routine memorized, and knows that

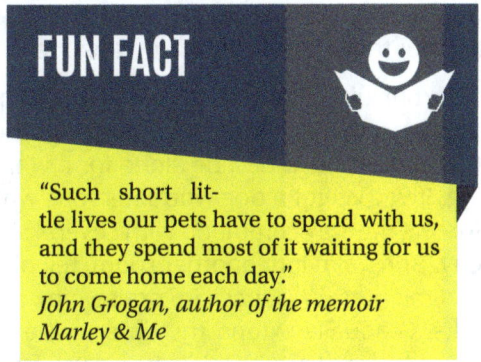

FUN FACT

"Such short little lives our pets have to spend with us, and they spend most of it waiting for us to come home each day."
John Grogan, author of the memoir Marley & Me

as soon as you close that door, if she starts to cry, whimper, or bark, you'll come running back, immediately showering her with attention and hugs. Every time you get ready to leave, she winds herself up for the pitch. The barking gets louder, the crying lasts longer. What's a dog parent to do?

My first dog was a very sweet, very spoiled Cocker Spaniel named Sherman. Any time we left Sherman alone in the house, he would howl. And howl. And howl. We lived in an apartment building at the time, the neighbors in the building knew when we were out, the neighbors from 4 blocks away knew when we were out, and it seemed that no matter how hard we tried to stop the howling, Sherman would have none of it. Whether we were downstairs for a quick trip to get the mail, or away for 3 hours, it didn't matter. The howling just intensified. Finally, we realized that Sherman was lonely. We left on the television, supplied him with all sorts of interesting chew toys, spent a small fortune on Nylabones and stuffed animals, and totally ignored him as we left the house. It worked. Sherman was busy, the howling ceased, and peace was once again restored to the neighborhood. But it wasn't easy.

Sherman wasn't a nervous, timid, or anxious dog. He was confident, happy, and otherwise a great canine companion. But being our first dog, he was more than a little spoiled, and he knew exactly how to push our buttons. His separation anxiety was most definitely a learned behavior.

If your dog is experiencing overall nervousness, has gone through changes in living arrangements, or is generally a timid dog, then her separation anxiety should be considered very real, and not something she's learned to do in order to get your attention. She's afraid to be alone. Often, dogs with genuine separation anxiety disorder are dogs who tend to never let their owners out of their sight, follow them from room to room, and panic when left alone. Some dog breeds in particular are more prone to separation anxiety than others. Fortunately, Airedale Terriers are not high on that list, but that's not to say it won't happen.

Your ultimate goal in easing the separation anxiety is to instill confidence and independence in your dog, and to have a dog who understands that even though he'll be alone for a while, he'll know that you'll be returning. If you've got a dog who's nervous when you leave the room, start reinforcing the stay command with several short, fun, rewarding sessions every day. Bring him into another room, tell him "stay," and leave him there for a few minutes. Walk back in, praise him, give him a treat and some vigorous pats. Gradually extend the time you're away from him. You can also give him a toy to play with while he's away from you—something new or a tasty, stuffed rubber bone to distract him and keep him occupied.

When he starts to realize that being away from your side is not such a bad thing, try this same process and leave the house. Don't make a big fuss about leaving, or returning. It may be difficult, but you'll need to simply ignore him. If he's usually in his crate when you leave, ask him to go into the

Photo Courtesy of Daniel Morgan

crate, give him a toy or a treat (a "high value" toy/treat works well here), and casually walk out of the house. (If there's typically TV or radio noise in the home, leave him with some music or a television show playing in the background. Classical music is nice for a bit of a soothing touch.)

Another "trick" to dealing with separation anxiety is to alter your routine. Your dog most likely knows what you're going to do before you know. She's got little else to do but study you, and she's well aware that when you pick up your purse, take out your car keys, and put on your red jacket that you're about to leave her alone, get in the car, and off you go. So vary your usual behavior. Leave the keys in the garage where she won't see you pick them up. Wear a different jacket. Leave your purse at home. Change it up! The less time she has to work herself into a dither, the easier it will be to leave. You don't have to wait until you've got one foot out the door before you offer her that high value toy. Try giving it to her, hang out in the house for a few minutes while she's munching on her toy or stuffed bone, then exit without any fanfare. Don't even say good-bye. When you return, again, no big deal, no fussing over your fur baby. You're here, she's here, it's all good.

We always hope that the solution to a dog's separation anxiety will be uncomplicated, but sometimes, no matter how hard we try, it still doesn't work. A professional dog trainer who is familiar with this behavioral issue can be a very good resource, and can provide help for you and your dog. There are also anti-anxiety medications for extreme separation issues, so if necessary, consult with your veterinarian for recommendations.

Digging

Airedales are notorious diggers. It may be attributable to their days as rodent hunters, when the breed was in its early stages. But whatever the reason, if you value your landscaping and your garden, or just don't relish the idea of falling into a 4-foot-deep sinkhole that didn't exist the last time you walked through your yard, we'd like to offer a heads-up here. Do not leave your Airedale outside unsupervised! An Airedale will dig when she's bored, tired, hot, cold, hasn't had enough exercise, has had too much exercise, smells something interesting, needs a shady spot to relax, or just because she's in the mood to dig. Our lovely fenced-in yard resembled the surface of the moon after our Airedale, Murphy, arrived on the scene. Miraculously, no one broke an ankle or worse by falling into one of her "burrows," but it became an ongoing struggle to convince her that digging random holes was totally unacceptable.

We finally solved the problem by constant supervision when she was outdoors, working with her via a new "leave it" command (as in, "no digging") and by providing her with ONE acceptable area which we had roped off, so she could visually determine where it was okay to dig as much as her little Airedale heart desired. Success! Unfortunately, the chosen spot was adjacent to a lovely, huge rhododendron bush, which was never quite the same, but Murphy was happy, the digging was limited to one fairly unobtrusive location, and the grass finally grew back in the rest of the yard.

Barking at the Door

This one is a bit tricky, and unfortunately, it's an issue that most of us dog parents have had to deal with at one time or another. Some of us are successful, some of us just give up and accept it as a fact of dog life, and make our apologies whenever the doorbell rings. Here's where the issue gets sticky: You don't like your dog barking at everyone who comes to the door. BUT many of us actually appreciate that little bit of reassurance that if there was ever an unwanted visitor standing on the other side of the front door, we LIKE the idea that our dog may, just may, provide a little bit of protection. Even the tiniest dog has been known to deter a would-be robber. Your dog can't determine whom to bark at, so she barks at everyone. It's up to you to let her know when, if ever, her barking is acceptable.

You're about to add another command to her vocabulary. You can use "quiet," "no barking," or "stop" if you'd like, but in our home, the way we tell our dog not to bark when someone is at the front door is by simply saying, "friend." That tells her that we are safe, she doesn't need to protect us, we've got this. Then she gets a treat for complying. At the same time, we're reinforcing the fact that we are in charge, and she's done a good job listening.

What's most important in teaching a dog not to bark at the door, or to have her stop when told, is remembering to keep your own response quiet, low-key, and calm. It's best to never yell at your dog under any circumstances, but even more so when she's barking at the door. A loud voice reprimanding her will only serve to escalate the situation, and that's the last thing you'd want to do.

There are other suggestions that occasionally work in getting a dog to stop barking at the door, one of which is the element of surprise. We've known people who use spray bottles of water when the barking starts. A stream of cold water to the backside is sometimes just enough to distract a determined Airedale. Others use a soda can filled with pennies that's shak-

CHAPTER 13   Dealing with Unwanted Behavior - Your Dog's Bad Habits

Photo Courtesy of
Jacqueline Jacobs

en as a way of taking the dog's focus away from the door. Ignoring the barking is another tactic if your dog is simply looking for your attention. Letting your guest know ahead of time that the dog may bark, and asking them to ignore her can be a temporary solution. But good training, consistency, and positive reinforcement always offer the most permanent route to success over the "quick fix."

So how, exactly, do you teach a dog the "quiet" command? While it may seem odd, the best way is to teach her to "speak." Hold out a treat, say, "speak" and at some point, she'll get the idea and bark. Praise her, and give her the treat. Be consistent, patient, and positive. After she learns the "speak" command, begin working on "quiet." She'll then get her treat when you give her the "quiet" command and she complies. It sounds counterproductive, and it may take a while, but she'll get it.

There are several degrees of door barkers. The well-trained ones will stop when you ask them. The middle-of-the-road barkers will stop when they see that there's no threat from whoever is on the other side of the door.

Then there are the non-stop barkers who will continue to bark and thoroughly terrorize anyone who dares to invade into their territory. The latter group is the most difficult to work with, and we'd suggest that a professional dog obedience trainer be called in to help. However, we would also recommend that the best trainer to call in this situation is one who will work with you and your dog at your home. This is a territorial issue, so your dog needs to be protecting his own home in order for the training to be most effective.

Jumping

Of all the bad habits that a dog may develop, jumping is the one behavior that commonly annoys people the most. It's rude, it displays a lack of good manners, and it can be downright scary for the non–dog lover. The most effective method to alleviate this behavior is to totally ignore the dog until all four of his paws are firmly on the floor. If your Airedale Terrier insists on jumping on you as soon as you walk into the house, just continue to walk past and ignore him. Once he's settled down, you can praise him for good behavior, then give him a treat or a gentle pat on the head. But remember to keep your demeanor calm and quiet and avoid exciting him. Speak to him in a quiet voice so that he knows you're still happy to see him, but let him know that a jumping dog will be ignored.

If your dog has a habit of jumping on your guests as they walk through the door, keep a collar and leash on him when visitors are expected, and

CHAPTER 13   Dealing with Unwanted Behavior - Your Dog's Bad Habits

at the first sign of him getting ready to jump, gently pull him back. Give him a firm and calm "no jump" command. Once he's settled down, your guests may calmly greet him. It's good to recruit a willing volunteer to practice working on this when company's NOT expected.

Bad habits can begin quickly in puppies. Teenaged Airedales can develop poor etiquette as a means of garnering attention, coping with boredom, or simply testing to see how much will be tolerated. Older dogs may have come by their behavioral issues because previous owners just didn't know or care about the best way to remedy their dog's bad habits. But every day can be a new beginning for you and your Airedale, so have patience, let your dog know that you love him, and celebrate his successes, no matter how big or small.

Aggression

Some doggy bad habits are quite annoying but with the right training, knowledge, and positive reinforcement, a first-time dog parent can usually correct an unwanted behavior which their dog has begun to exhibit. Aggression issues, however, are best left to a professional dog trainer or dog behavioral specialist. That's not to say that an aggressive behavior can't be alleviated. Far from it. But if you're already seeing some tendencies toward growling, food possessiveness, territorial protectiveness, aggressiveness while on leash, or dog fights (whether minor or more serious), then we would highly recommend that you consult with a professional dog behavioral specialist.

Causes of aggression are many: your dog could be in pain and protecting himself from further injury. He may have come from a situation where he was attacked or bullied by another dog or abused by his former owner. He may be fearful or protecting what he perceives as his territory. He may have actually been taught to be aggressive. Food aggression could be the result of having to fight another dog for his share of a meal. Some dogs can show aggression when it comes to a favorite toy.

If you notice signs of aggression—growling, lunging toward another dog or human, showing teeth, nipping, snapping, biting (including bites that break skin as well as bites which leave a mark or bruise), or aggressive barking, then it's time to call in a specialist. It's a behavioral issue that can be remedied, but don't wait until an injury—or worse—occurs. Aggression toward another dog or a human should NEVER be ignored, excused, or tolerated.

Andrea BROWN BERMAN | The Complete Guide to Airedale Terriers

Photo Courtesy of Carly Kanipe

CHAPTER 14
Your Airedale Terrier's Health and Nutrition

"Plenty of exercise is required on daily basis. Basic habits in accordance with the pup's age should apply. We caution owners to be mindful of developing hips, to minimize jumping, and avoid smooth or tile floors."

Tony Hogg
North FL Airedales

Health Disorders

Like most purebred dogs, Airedale Terriers do have some known genetic disorders and can be prone to certain medical conditions. Overall, they are a relatively hardy breed, but for an Airedale parent, forewarned is forearmed. Among the most common medical conditions seen in this breed are skin allergies, autoimmune diseases, hypothyroidism, kidney disease, certain cancers, cataracts, bloat, Addison's disease, Cushing's disease, hip and knee dysplasia, constipation and bowel irregularities, and heart abnormalities. There are other diseases and disorders that are considered to be inherent in the Airedale breed, but of course, that doesn't indicate that your Airedale will acquire any of those. Every year, we're told that a certain strain of the flu will be going around, so we need to be on the lookout and be aware. Will we be among those who contract a particular virus? Not necessarily, but it's good to be informed.

FUN FACT
Rawhide Cautions

Choosing the right rawhide for your dog can be a tricky task. The AKC recommends choosing rawhides that are made domestically and rinsing rawhide bones before giving them to your dog. Rawhide isn't easily digestible and can present a choking or obstruction risk if large, unchewed sections are swallowed. For more information about the risks and digestability of rawhide bones, speak with your veterinarian.

If you've purchased your dog from an Airedale breeder, your pet most likely would have been tested for hip and cardiac conditions and renal disease, and have had ophthalmology exams, all of which are dog breed health testing requirements of the American Kennel Club (AKC) for breeders of Airedale Terriers. Your veterinarian should also be familiar with the Airedale Terrier, and know what health issues are inherent in the breed.

The Importance of Regular Veterinary Visits

Every Airedale parent should be aware of the importance of visiting their dog's veterinary practice on a regular basis to maintain their pet's ongoing good health. Besides vaccinations, booster shots, immunizations, and annual check-ups, any questions or concerns regarding a dog's health and well-being should always be addressed sooner rather than later. Procrastinating over what may be thought to be a minor health issue could lead to more serious consequences. Don't rely on the internet when it comes to your dog's health concerns. Pick up the phone, make an appointment to have your Airedale evaluated by your veterinarian, and respect his or her professional experience.

New dog parents will usually be given a schedule for all of the testing, inoculations, routine exams, medications, and laboratory work that dogs will need on an annual basis. Heartworm, flea and tick treatments, para-

Photo Courtesy of Ruth Antoniuk

site testing, dental exams, weight checks, and spay and neuter discussions and scheduling should all be part of your dog's veterinary visit. Additionally, you'll be asked about your Airedale's daily routine, which should address nutritional needs, urinary and bowel schedules, behavioral and exercise routines, socialization, training, and overall temperament. Your vet wants your dog to be healthy from a physical standpoint, but will also want to know that he's getting along well in the household and in his general environment. No question or concern should be considered irrelevant on your part, so don't hesitate to ask.

Pet Insurance

There is no correct answer as to whether or not you should have pet insurance for your Airedale. There are those who absolutely would not be without it, and an equal number of pet parents who wouldn't even consider it.

Annual pet insurance costs vary, from a quoted low of $10 per month to upwards of $100 per month and more. Coverage differs as well, so a vast amount of research is recommended. If you're considering a policy, it's especially important to speak with your veterinary practice to find out what they recommend and whether they accept a particular insurance, as well as inquire as to what coverage is offered. Is there a deductible? Are routine exams covered? Is there an annual maximum coverage? Is the insurance ap-

CHAPTER 14   Your Airedale Terrier's Health and Nutrition

plicable to chronic illnesses, accidents, medications? What about pre-existing conditions? Are there claim caps, discounts for yearly well-being exams and ongoing treatments such as heartworm medications and flea/tick treatments? What is their percentage of reimbursement? Do the yearly premiums increase as the dog gets older? Are genetic conditions covered? Is there a wait time to begin coverage? Is training for behavioral treatment covered? Multiple pet discounts?

Some homeowners and automobile insurers offer pet insurance as a bundle feature. Have you checked with your existing insurers to see if this is part of their coverage? Keep in mind that many pet insurance companies do not deal directly with veterinarians, but will reimburse you at a later date. Others, however, do work in partnership with veterinary practices. One major factor when contemplating the pet insurance puzzle: In the event of a catastrophic illness or accident, veterinary expenses can be astronomical, resulting in thousands of dollars of medical expenses. In a case such as this, pet insurance could be well worth the investment.

You can see that there are many aspects to consider when choosing whether or not to purchase pet insurance. Weigh the positives and negatives, research costs and coverages, and make an informed decision as to whether it's an option for you.

Grooming Requirements

There's no dog quite as beautiful as a well-groomed Airedale. Of course, that's a matter of opinion (mine), and I'm the first to admit a definite partiality to the breed. On the grooming spectrum, Airedale Terriers are not a particularly high-maintenance breed.

FUN FACT

"Anybody who doesn't know what soap tastes like never washed a dog." – Lee Iacocca

They do, however, need a good brushing several times a week, and should have a professional grooming every few months—approximately 4 to 6 times per year is recommended. Although many are under the impression that Airedales do not shed and are hypoallergenic, this is not true. They DO shed, although not in great quantities. The Airedale's coat is composed of two layers—a soft undercoat, and a coarse, wiry topcoat. Due to this breed's propensity toward dry or

113

sensitive skin and some dermatological issues, it's actually recommended that they not be groomed and/or brushed excessively.

Other grooming should include good dental hygiene, as well as regular ear cleaning and trimming the hair inside their ears when necessary. This will ensure proper air circulation in order to avoid possible ear infections caused by dampness. Never use cotton-tip swabs on your Airedale. Use only cotton balls or a soft washcloth, and avoid pushing anything into their ear canals. Their shaggy beards typically need frequent attention in the form of washing after meals—a wet washcloth will do the job.

In the paw department, pads should be trimmed of fur and nails clipped as needed. If your Airedale spends most of his time walking on grass as opposed to concrete, nail clipping may need to be done more often as sidewalks and streets will wear down the nails more quickly than soft surfaces. One peculiar trait that I have found with Airedales is that they seem to have much more sensitive feet than some other breeds. It's always advisable to get them accustomed to nail clipping, pad trimming, and regular grooming from an early age.

When considering a professional groomer, check references, licenses, and certifications. Look for a facility that is clean, with staff that's welcoming, knowledgeable, and professional. Be sure that they are familiar with the Airedale breed, and what the grooming standards are. If you know other Airedale parents, ask for recommendations. Not only are you looking for a professional who knows how to groom an Airedale, but equally important is finding a groomer who is familiar with the breed's temperament.

If you live in an area where ticks are present, be on the lookout for these nasty little buggers. They will burrow their way into your dog's skin, and because of your Airedale's coarse coat, may go unnoticed. A thorough inspection during tick season should be done whenever your dog has been in grassy or wooded areas, or around other dogs. Fleas and ticks can jump from one dog to another quite easily. Be diligent about checking the fur around your dog's paws as well as all other areas of his body. Many a dog has stepped into a tick nest and subsequently carried a few generations of ticks into the home. During tick season, make it a habit to give your dog's coat and skin a thorough inspection before entering the house. Whenever you're out for a walk with your Airedale, carry tweezers with you for an emergency tick removal.

CHAPTER 14 Your Airedale Terrier's Health and Nutrition

Your Airedale Terrier's Nutrition

"We recommend high quality food, preferably grain free, as we see better coats and health. Cheap food often results in skin allergies and much larger poops. Airedale's can make surprisingly big poops!"

Tony Hog
North FL Airedales

If your Airedale is a puppy, your breeder will have already begun feeding her a nutritionally complete food that's appropriate for puppies. Your veterinarian will likely recommend that you continue to feed your dog the diet with which she's already familiar. Whatever food your dog is eating should contain the proper balance of vitamins, minerals, carbohydrates, fats, and proteins for her age, weight, and energy level. You'll need to modify amounts and feeding times as your dog develops and matures, but it's always best to consult with your veterinarian when making any changes. The brands and ingredients available are numerous. Equally important is whether your dog has any particular sensitivities. If she has food allergies, a sensitive stomach, is higher or lower energy, or has any dietary restrictions, these considerations must all be factored into her feeding routine. Affordability as well as availability of dog food brands should also be taken into account. Any changes in her diet must be done on a very gradual basis.

Just as your dog will have preferences as to the types of food she's enjoying, you should also give some thought as to your own dietary requirements and how these will affect your dog. Do you prefer a more holistic regimen? Do you cook all of your own food from scratch? Do you and your family consume only organically based foods? Is your diet exclusively vegetarian or vegan?

You always have the option of serving your dog only home-cooked meals, as many pet parents prefer to do, thus eliminating fillers, chemicals, and by-products. However, even though you may think your dog is eating a healthier, more nutritious diet, it may not be the case. Your dog does need a balanced diet, so let your veterinarian know what you're cooking for your Airedale. She may recommend that you include some additional vitamins or supplements in your dog's daily regimen.

Whether you're cooking for your pet and feeding her homemade meals or giving her people food as an occasional treat, you should always be aware of which foods are agreeing with her, are good for her health, or are just not appropriate. There are many recipes available, both online and in specialized dog recipe cookbooks, geared toward homemade dog foods and dog treats. But all should initially be given to your dog in moderation, to avoid stomach upsets and digestive issues or allergic reactions.

Photo Courtesy of Charlee Ackley

Some human foods that dogs usually enjoy include cooked chicken and meats, salmon, peanut butter, cheese, plain unsweetened yogurt, cottage cheese, cooked vegetables such as carrots, sweet potatoes, green beans, broccoli, pumpkin, squash, peas, apple slices, bananas, oatmeal, rice, tuna, and cooked eggs. Foods that you should avoid feeding your dog include acidic foods such as tomatoes, citrus fruits, grapes and raisins, chocolate, onions, garlic, bread dough, nuts, processed deli meats, any foods with a high sugar or salt content, and soft bones or bones that are small enough to splinter or lodge in your Airedale's throat.

Probiotics for Dogs

Some dogs have chronic or occasional digestive problems. I am personally familiar with this issue, as my own rescue dog, who is quite healthy and hardy in most respects, has been known to have bouts of intestinal upheaval every once in a while. Her regular diet includes a nutritionally balanced dry dog food, a treat or two at various times during the day, and a few appropriate human food scraps left over from our nightly dinner. I might mix several teaspoons of chicken, vegetables, or meat into her dry food, as she loves a little variety. However, every now and then, for no apparent reason, she'd have some intestinal distress in the form of diarrhea or constipation. We had visited our veterinarian on several of these occasions just to be sure there was no serious cause for alarm, but after some routine testing, the vet recommended a daily dose of a probiotic for her, which we implemented immediately after that appointment. This was approximately two years ago, and she has not had another occurrence of digestive upset since.

If your dog suffers from occasional (or more frequent) stomach upsets, it's important to consult with your veterinarian. Probiotic supplements are not recommended for dogs with severely compromised immune systems or for very young puppies. The risks and side effects of probiotics with otherwise healthy dogs have been reported as minimal. It is not recommended that dogs ingest probiotics that are made for humans.

Research into the use of dog probiotic supplements is still ongoing, but it's been reported that many dogs have been found to benefit, not only with digestive issues and bowel function, but also with skin allergies, infections, bad breath, excessive gas, and even some diseases and disorders. Dog probiotics can be found in pill form, chewable tablets, or powders, and costs will vary depending upon brand and dosage. My dog takes a daily powdered probiotic which comes in individual packets. I add one packet in with her dry food, along with a bit of warm water. Cost-wise, each packet is less than one dollar. Dog probiotics may be purchased on the internet and in pet stores, and most veterinarians who recommend them will have them available as well.

Airedale Terriers as Therapy Dogs

Although any well-trained dog with excellent manners and great social skills has the potential to be a wonderful therapy dog, an Airedale Terrier has something special that not all dogs possess: he's a comedian. He has an innate ability to make people smile. He's well aware of the fact that he's totally adorable, his curls make him irresistibly pettable, and his intelligence and intuitive abilities are second to none. So if you've been thinking that your Airedale would excel as a therapy dog, you may be correct.

Before you go walking into the nearest nursing facility or public building with your lovable Airedale in tow, there are some things to note. There is a huge difference between service dogs and therapy dogs. Service dogs are canines that are highly trained to help their owners with specific tasks. They work as a team with owners who face the challenges of various disabilities, including hearing and vision impairment, autism, seizures, diabetes, PTSD, mobility and emotional disorders, and other physical and mental limitations. These dogs are legally allowed to accompany their owners anywhere that their owners go, from places of employment to schools, hospitals, retail businesses, and other establishments.

Photo Courtesy of Beth Pagan

Owners of therapy dogs, on the other hand, work with their dogs for the purpose of helping others, whether that's to bring a smile to the face of a nursing home resident, visiting children in a hospital or school, or visiting an assisted living facility, a hospice facility, or an area where victims of a disaster have been housed. Some airports are now bringing in therapy dogs to ease the stress that travelers invariably exhibit due to delayed or cancelled flights or unforeseen travel circumstances. The Americans with Disabilities Act does not recognize therapy dogs as service dogs.

What qualities should your dog possess to be considered a good candidate as a therapy dog? Unquestionably, she must have a great temperament. She should be in excellent health, calm, friendly, well-mannered, and able to tolerate sudden movement by strangers who may need to physically move in ways in which a dog may not be generally accustomed. (Note: Your Airedale should also be quite "surefooted." Hospitals and nursing facilities are known to have slippery, shiny, waxed floors. With some dogs, no matter how calm and gentle they are, this may be a potential concern. I can attest to this, courtesy of a perfect-in-every-other-way Airedale who simply could not manage to stay upright on the waxed surface of a nursing home floor.)

Your aspiring therapy Airedale should enjoy being petted and cuddled, know and respond to basic commands, walk well on a leash without pulling, not be fearful of loud noises or sudden motion, or startled by equipment such as wheelchairs, stretchers, canes, or crutches. They should love people, and be confident, gentle, and good listeners. Any dog can be a great companion and amazing friend, but it takes a very special dog, and a very special owner, to bring a bit of comfort to those who are facing physical and emotional challenges.

CHAPTER 14 Your Airedale Terrier's Health and Nutrition

There are many organizations which can provide information and resources to help you decide if your Airedale Terrier would be a good therapy dog, and offer classes, certifications, and training. Internet sites are a good place to start researching what's available in your area. Many dog obedience trainers also offer programs in Canine Good Citizenship and therapy dog training. There are no "official" certifications or licenses for your dog to become a therapy dog, but many facilities WILL require a certification from a recognized therapy dog organization before you will be allowed to bring your dog in to visit. If you think you and your Airedale have what it takes to become a therapy dog team, contact one of these organizations to learn what's involved in their training programs. They can help you on your journey to bring a little sunshine into someone's life.

> **FUN FACT**
> **Assistance Dogs International**
>
> Assistance Dogs International (ADI) was formed in 1986 and is a worldwide organization that accredits programs that train assistance dogs. The ADI does not train or certify service animals, but it maintains a database of organizations that provide these services. For more information, visit their website.

CHAPTER 15
Your Aging Airedale

When is your dog officially considered a "senior citizen"? For the Airedale Terrier breed, with an average life expectancy of 10 to 13 years, it's when he's approximately seven and a half years of age. Although your Airedale won't qualify for Medicare or Social Security anytime soon, and he may not be on the AARP mailing list, one day you'll realize that your Airedale is no longer a spunky, young pup. Take heart. These are the best years of your lives together, so enjoy every minute with your adorable, fuzzy canine companion. He may be slowing down a bit, his needs may be quite different from what they were when he was a youngster, but his loyalty and love, and that incomparable Airedale spirit, are still very much present.

CHAPTER 15　Your Aging Airedale

The Older Airedale's Health

Whether your Airedale Terrier has been part of your family since he was a puppy or you adopted a teenager, a more mature dog, or (bless you!) a senior Airedale in need of a loving home for the remaining years of his life, you'll find that your dog's advancing age necessitates changes; some will be minor, others, more considerable.

This is an important time to remember to schedule annual veterinary visits for your dog. Of course, if there is an emergency, or if something about your Airedale just seems a bit "off," you'll need more urgent medical guidance, but routine check-ups are an essential part of your dog's physical as well as mental health during his senior years. Medications and supplements that are recommended by your veterinarian can prolong your dog's life, and could mean the difference between continued good health for your Airedale or unnecessary discomfort.

Some genetic disorders of Airedale Terriers can be addressed if found early enough. A vet who is familiar with the breed will be aware of conditions that are hereditary, and will be knowledgeable with regard to treatment. Cataracts, digestive disorders, heart disease, pancreatitis, Cushing's and Addison's diseases, cancer, canine dementia, allergies, tremors, neurologic and thyroid disorders, and bone and joint concerns are sometimes seen in older Airedales. Dental disease and obesity can also be common to Airedales as they age.

Your dog's exercise routine may be changing, but daily walks, outdoor time, and socialization are as necessary for an older dog as they are for a puppy. The quantity may be less, but the quality can be every bit as much fun as ever. Check with your vet before adding any new or increased physical activities to your dog's exercise schedule, and remember that moderation should be a key factor. In your dog's older age, you and he may have been slowing things down, so don't put the pedal to the metal and give your dog a workout that's beyond his physical capabilities. If you have access to a beach or lake, and your Airedale enjoys a swim or even a walk in shallow water, a dog with osteoarthritis may benefit greatly. A senior Airedale may not have the stamina for as much activity as he once did, but low-impact exercise and shorter walks could be just what the doctor orders.

And please don't forget that your Airedale's need for mental stimulation is likely as strong as ever, so invent some games for him to keep his mind active: hide and seek with treats, interactive dog toys, easy walks to new places, and exposure to a variety of sights, smells and sounds that he's never experienced before. You CAN teach an old dog new tricks.

Many senior dogs benefit from supplements such as glucosamine and chondroitin both to relieve pain and stiffness from previous injuries or joint inflammation, and as a preventative treatment. Urinary tract infections can also be prevalent in older dogs with already compromised immune systems. Although UTIs are more frequent in female dogs, older male dogs can also be susceptible. If your senior dog is experiencing discomfort upon urination, more frequent urination, or if there is evidence of blood in her urine, a visit to the vet should be on your to-do immediately list. It could be a bacterial infection, or it could indicate something more serious.

In addition to medications and vitamin and joint supplements, there are many other therapeutic measures to help keep your senior dog happy, healthy, and comfortable, including massage, hydro/water therapy, acupuncture or acupressure, chiropractic treatment, laser therapy, and physical therapy. Consult with your veterinarian for recommendations specific to your Airedale's individual needs.

If your older dog has become less active, but is still eating the same food in the same amounts as he always did, he could be a candidate for many preventable conditions caused by obesity. In other words, is your dog getting fat? If the answer is a resounding "YES!" it may be time to get Mr. Airedale back on track with some dietary and nutritional adjustments that suit his current more sedentary lifestyle. Airedale Terriers are predisposed to putting on excessive weight in their senior years, so dog parents should remain vigilant. What might seem like "just a few extra pounds" to you could be putting your dog at risk for heart disease, joint, bone, and muscle damage, increased blood pressure, surgical complications, and respiratory distress, among a host of other potential problems. Your veterinarian can advise on the best dietary plan for your dog, based on activity level, nutritional needs, and physical condition. In the meantime, if you notice that your dog is putting on the pounds, it won't hurt in the least to be proactive and begin to implement some healthier habits.

It's easy enough to cut back on between-meal snacks, or substitute some cooked baby carrots or other vegetables instead of the usual dog treats. If you're a pet parent who loves to whip up some healthy, homemade snacks for your dog, consider purchasing a dehydrator. There's no limit to the tasty, crunchy, nutritious snacks you can make for your favorite Airedale, and at a fraction of the cost and calories of store-bought products: dried apple slices, the crunchy "jerky" treats that dogs love (think chicken or turkey strips), dried fish nuggets from tuna or salmon, sweet potato slices, dehydrated banana bites. Dehydrators can be inexpensive, use minimal electricity, and the possibilities are endless for your dog (and for your humans as well!).

CHAPTER 15   Your Aging Airedale

Simple Adjustments

Your senior Airedale may be trying to tell you that he needs a bit of assistance to keep him comfortable and allow him to continue to enjoy life's little pleasures. Where he might have once bolted into the car to head out for a ride as soon as he saw you putting on your coat, he now may be hesitating. "Mommy, my legs hurt, and that's a big jump." Where he once slept peacefully on the family room sofa, he could be spending more time napping on the carpet or in his bed. He might not be quite so excited to go out for walks as he once was. He may need a helping hand.

FUN FACT

In 2019, a sculpture to commemorate Airedale terriers and the soldiers they served with during WWI was begun. The memorial is being sculpted from a 30-ton block of granite and will stand at East Haven Beach in Carnoustie, England, where Lt. Col. Edwin Richardson, who trained Airedales during WWI, lived. The sculpture is expected to be unveiled before the end of 2019.

A car ramp is a great accessory to accommodate your older Airedale's changing mobility. Ramps are lightweight, foldable, simple to transport, and will make it easier for your dog to continue to travel and enjoy car rides with his family. Ramps are available with non-slip surfaces, and many can be adjusted to allow for easy access to either vehicle or sofa height.

Your dog's grooming needs will change as she gets older. She may develop dry and/or itchy skin which could be due to vitamin deficiencies or allergies. Her coat may become dull, and more easily matted. Daily "bump" checks are essential, as senior dogs can develop a variety of lesions and growths. Crusty patches, warts, fatty tumors, cysts, and other lumpy, bumpy skin conditions can frequently appear on an older Airedale's skin. Many of these are harmless and benign, but early detection of a potential health concern and a visit to the vet is always the best course of action. With careful inspection and regular doggy grooming sessions, you'll be alerted to any new skin issues that need attention.

Add an orthopedic bed to your dog's favorite sleeping spot. If your senior Airedale has been having difficulty climbing stairs, make first-floor accommodations fit for a king by providing him with a new doggy bed that will make him more comfortable when resting. Providing more support for his spine will decrease the stress on his joints and bones. Before you purchase an orthopedic bed for your dog, consider how he sleeps. Does he like to stretch out? Is he happier curled up in a big ball? For reasons we'll never know, many Airedales love to sleep with their heads hanging down over a bolster, pillow, or the edge of a mattress. Your senior will greatly appreciate a restful snooze on a bed that fits his favorite sleeping style while soothing his achy bones.

As your dog ages, you may notice changes in his behavior. Some can be quite apparent, others more subtle. Just as the aging human will eventually experience some loss of mobility, hearing and/or vision deterioration, and all of the other accoutrements that appear on the senior citizen spectrum, an older Airedale will undergo changes as well. If your Airedale is in pain or physically uncomfortable in any way, your previous Mr. Personality may now be Mr. Grumpy. If he's suddenly not listening to you, he may have a hearing loss. Older dogs can experience incontinence, exhibit a change in temperament, forget commands, and have an increase or decrease in appetite. They may want more cuddles or less snuggles, require more sleep or become restless. They may seem more anxious and fearful than usual, become confused and forgetful, and could be more sensitive to extreme weather conditions. In colder climates, your senior Airedale NEEDS a cozy, fleecy coat to protect him from the elements, but even with warm outerwear, try not to take him outside for extended periods of time. In hot weather, your Airedale would enjoy the benefits of air conditioning, a plastic kiddie pool located in a shady spot to relax in and cool off, and shorter times outdoors in the heat.

Photo Courtesy of Brad Peas

There are other transformations that your dog might experience as he grows older. It's all part of an Airedale's natural aging process, and again, your veterinarian is your best resource in helping to ensure that your dog enjoys a long and happy life. With your patience, awareness, and a continued commitment to his good health and well-being, your Airedale will always know that he's in good hands, and that he's pawsitively loved and adored.

CHAPTER 15   Your Aging Airedale

When It's Time to Say Good-bye

Few things in this world are as heartbreaking as having to say good-bye to your beloved dog. But there comes a time when you just know. We can't make it easier or take away the sadness, or give you the strength to make the decision to say farewell. We can't offer you the right words to let you know that you've done what was best for your dog. We can only tell you that one day, your heart will begin to heal, and you'll remember all the joy and little blessings that this furry kid brought to you. If only our Airedales could stay with us forever.

There are ways that you'll know when "that time" has come: if your Airedale is in pain, if he's no longer eating and drinking, if his body is no longer functioning as it should, if he's having trouble standing and walking, if his quality of life has deteriorated. If he's been in an accident or injured and it's unlikely that he'll recover, if he's been suffering from an illness from which the prognosis is poor. Listen to your heart.

Think back to that first day when your Airedale came into your life. You made the decision that a puppy would be the perfect addition to your household. Or you adopted a dog who was in need of a new home. You anticipated her arrival by preparing and planning, so you'd know what to expect. Now it's once again time to prepare.

Your veterinarian is there to offer you the guidance and advice that you will need.

He will explain the process of euthanasia. Veterinarians are professionals—knowledgeable about the patients they treat, but compassionate, caring human beings who understand what you are going through. As you begin to comprehend this somber chapter of your dog's life, here's a bit of information in which you may find some small amount of solace: The word "euthanasia" comes from the Greek words meaning "gentle and easy death."

Many vets will come to a patient's home when a dog is to be euthanized. Home euthanasia may not be the best choice for everyone, but if this is an option for you and your dog, discuss it with your pet's doctor as well as with your household members. Some may prefer a clinical setting over the home environment.

There are additional decisions to be made besides when and where. Many of us opt to be beside our pets as we say our final good-bye. We want our dogs to know that we're with them, comforting them until the end. But others will find it much too difficult to be there. It's a very personal choice, and if you feel that being present is not something that you can do, then don't. It's not necessary to explain or make excuses to anyone. It's the best decision for you and for your dog. End of discussion. Again, listen to your heart.

In most cases, a veterinarian will administer a sedative to your dog before giving her an injection of pentobarbital, which will cause her heart to slow down and ultimately stop beating. Your beloved Airedale will be at peace. Your veterinarian will discuss post-euthanasia arrangements with you, and explain cremation, burial, and the choices you can make which will be the most comforting for you and your family.

There's no doubt that the loss of a pet leaves a hole in your heart. It's all part of the grieving process. Treasure the memories.

There are many grief support groups available to help those who have experienced the sorrow of losing a beloved pet. They can offer assistance if you need someone to talk to, and guide you through these difficult days. Your veterinarian may be able to provide information on how to contact an organization or professional who specializes in pet grief support, and there are many resources available online. Just know that when the time comes, you are not alone, and that others are there for you. Anyone who has ever loved and lost a pet will understand the sadness that you are experiencing. A favorite quote that I've recounted far too often, but one that I cherish nonetheless is by author A.A. Milne and his beloved Winnie the Pooh: "How lucky I am to have something that makes saying good-bye so hard".

In addition to the condolences, sympathy, and kind words you'll receive, you will invariably be asked, probably numerous times, "When are you going to get another dog?" People mean well with their inquiries, but often it's much too painful to think about, let alone discuss. There's no easy or correct answer, and only you and your family will know when...and if...the time is right to welcome another dog into your home. For me, personally, whenever I have had to say good-bye to my best furry friend (and there have been many), I have always said, "I can't go through this again. It's just too difficult. No more dogs!"

But then, somewhere in the middle of the grief and emptiness that I'm feeling, I realize that the best tribute I can give to my beloved canine companion is to rescue another dog who needs a good home and a caring family. And when I'm ready, and I meet that precious furry kid who licks my face and melts my heart, it will be the perfect time to give love another chance. And so it begins, all over again.

CHAPTER 15   Your Aging Airedale

The Beginning

The Complete Guide to Airedale Terriers has taken you on a journey throughout all of the stages of this incomparable breed of dog, from the ups and downs of puppyhood, to the challenges of the teenager phase, to your dog's more tranquil senior years. No book can accurately answer the question of what life with your own unique dog will be like. Will your dog be energetic? A couch potato? Will she be a happy-go-lucky free spirit, a sophisticated, independent lady? A serious old soul? A rambunctious and rowdy goofball?

Photo Courtesy of Kelly Scollin

Her lineage as a puppy, or her past history or experiences as an older dog, may give you some clues as to what to expect as you begin your life together. You'll discover characteristics that no other dog possesses. You'll wonder at your Airedale's penchant for tennis balls, his obsession with chasing chipmunks, laugh at the way he marches in place when you scratch his back, sigh in frustration when he devours the leftover meatloaf on the kitchen counter. You'll question whether he will ever be totally housetrained. (He will.) You'll rejoice in his intuitive ability to bring sunshine into the dark days, and admire his good listening skills when you need a non-judgmental opinion. And although we've tried our best to address many of the questions about what living with an Airedale Terrier will be like, we really can't answer the most important question of all…

How did you ever live without him?

Although you've reached the end of this book, we hope that it's just the beginning of your amazing and awesome Airedale Adventure!

Andrea BROWN BERMAN | The Complete Guide to Airedale Terriers

From their perky little ears to their stubby little tails
There's no dog in the world like our precious Airedales.
Confidence and attitude, you surely can't deny,
Innocence in his angelic face, with a twinkle in his eye.
A clown, an athlete, yet stubborn as a mule,
He's the "A-plus" student at obedience school.
He'll dig in your garden, destroy all your plants.
His nickname should be Mr. Smartypants.
A joyous party animal, he loves to whoop it up,
There's certainly a zest for life, with this happy, playful pup.
Trouble is often his middle name.
"Outsmarting my human" his favorite game.
A loving soul, beyond compare,
He'll steal your heart, so just beware.
Life's never dull with an Airedale, you'll find.
With mischief, he's truly a mastermind.
His antics will keep you entertained,
On commands, your Airedale's got you well-trained.
At snuggling and cuddling, this dog is an ace,
He can easily put a smile on your face.
He's devoted and loyal, his love has no end,
You're his leader, his guardian, his hero, his friend.
If you'd just like to know how to make your life merrier,
The solution is simple—it's a sweet Airedale Terrier.

***

This book is dedicated to Murphy,
a very special little girl

www.ingramcontent.com/pod-product-compliance
Lightning Source LLC
Chambersburg PA
CBHW060043230426
43661CB00004B/642